More Worlds to Negotiate

John Dunlop and the Art of Problem Solving

More Worlds to Negotiate

John Dunlop and the Art of Problem Solving

Jennifer C. Berkshire

Hamilton Books

Lanham • Boulder • New York • Toronto • London

Published by Hamilton Books
An imprint of The Rowman & Littlefield Publishing Group, Inc.
4501 Forbes Boulevard, Suite 200, Lanham, Maryland 20706
Hamilton Books Acquisitions Department (301) 459-3366

6 Tinworth Street, London SE11 5AL, United Kingdom

Printed in the United States of America

British Library Cataloguing in Publication Information Available

Library of Congress Control Number: 2010929916
ISBN: 978-0-7618-7112-5 (cloth)
ISBN: 978-0-7618-7259-7 (pbk)
ISBN: 978-0-7618-7113-2 (electronic)

Contents

Acknowledgments

It is a cliche to proclaim that a book wouldn't exist without a collective's-worth of effort. But with this book, it really is the case. I first encountered John Dunlop, the problem-solver, when I was asked to prepare a teaching case for the Harvard Labor and Worklife Program, the contemporary iteration of the Harvard Trade Union Program that Dunlop helped to establish more than seven decades ago. The case chronicled Dunlop's effort to negotiate a lasting peace between migrant farmworkers, who had no labor protections to speak of, and Campbell Soup, the target of a years-long boycott for its treatment of the workers who picked tomatoes and other crops for the food processing giant. I came away feeling deeply impressed by the deft way in which Dunlop had managed to balance competing interests, setting up the architecture for a structure, known as the Dunlop Commission, which not only lives on today but has expanded to include some 10,000 migrant farmworkers who travel to the US each year to work in the fields of North Carolina.

So when I was approached with an offer to write a book about John Dunlop's problem-solving work, I leaped at the chance. Of course, producing the volume required first solving a problem—a rather significant one as I'd learn. Dunlop left behind an impressive *oeuvre* as an academic economist, weighty tomes with titles like *Industrial Relations Systems* that were now stacked up in my office. But of his non-academic work, the arbitrating and negotiating, the persuasion and defusing, there was virtually nothing. Well, nothing on paper. The record existed in the memories of his colleagues, both in and out of academia, former students, and the many individuals whom he mentored over the decades. Writing a book about Dunlop's practical work, as he referred to it, would require the extensive assistance of the people who'd partnered with him in an astonishing number of endeavors.

Their names appear throughout this volume, but they deserve special mention here. David Weil, Fred Abernathy, John Read, Kris Rondeau, Jon Brock, Baldemar Velásquez, Ray Goldberg, Karen Ignagni, Arnold Zack, Tom Kochan and Derek Bok spent countless hours walking me through Dunlop's effort to address some seemingly intractable problem—soaring inflation in the 70's, student and labor unrest at Harvard, threats to U.S. manufacturing in a globalizing economy, just to name a few. Elaine Bernard, in her role as the director of the Harvard Labor and Worklife Program, was endlessly supportive of the project, helping me to track down any lead regarding Dunlop's work, no matter how obscure. Her wisdom and insight regarding what Dunlop understood as the "personal ingredient" within labor unions and the academy helped me navigate institutions that I never would have been able to on my own. And Beverly Donohue, Dunlop's daughter, paid me the ultimate compliment by entrusting me with the personal diary that her father kept while in office as secretary of labor in the Ford Administration.

During the months that I had the privilege of working with what was in essence Dunlop's extended family, I felt at times that I was part of it. While I'd never sat through an endless negotiating session with him, or been on the receiving end of one of Dunlop's rules for conducting business—like when to show up for a meeting (exactly three to four minutes early), or how to work the room at a cocktail party (counterclockwise, two minutes per person)—the willingness of his compatriots to share these stories and many, many more let me imagine that I had.

My own family deserves some recognition as well. I inherited my curious nature, which I've parlayed into a passion for interviewing and story telling from my father, Tom Berkshire. And my husband and intellectual sparring partner, Russ Davis, is an invaluable source of support and advice, some of which I take. Finally, I owe a debt of gratitude to the subject of this volume: John Dunlop himself. As I worked to capture the spirit of his problem-solving work on the page, I often felt as though the "mechanisms" he was forever creating were also influencing me. Five decades ago, Dunlop expressed alarm that Americans were retreating to "islands of self-interest" that would make it all but impossible to solve pressing national problems. I wrote this book from my home in Gloucester, Massachusetts, a literal island; in these intensely tribal times I'm often on a figurative island too. Dunlop leaves behind a legacy of bridge building and an inspiring example to follow. Spouting opinions is easy, as he liked to point out, but the real work lies in changing minds.

Introduction

What Would Dunlop Do?

The mood at John Dunlop's swearing in as President Ford's new secretary of labor was festive. The ceremony, held on March 18, 1975 in the East Room of the White House, was packed with representatives from seemingly every labor union, a tribute to Dunlop's close ties to organized labor, as well as his lengthy career as a mediator. And yet Dunlop's words to the crowd were cautionary, even ominous. He used the ceremonial event to address what he saw as the weighty matters that were then confronting the nation, and the increasing tendency among policy makers to focus on the short term, rather than the longer-term interests of the country. "I tried to say a number of things of substance without being unduly offensive," he recalled in the personal diary he kept throughout his time in Washington.[1]

But Dunlop's sternest words were reserved for what he regarded as the creeping menace of over-regulation. He warned that government agencies were becoming increasingly heavy-handed, their regulations ever more detailed. Pursuing government by regulation rather than "by mediation, by catalysts, by persuasion," Dunlop warned, had gone so far as to be detrimental to the best interests of the country. It was a theme he would return to again and again during his ten months in office, using his place at the helm of a department with significant regulatory authority to caution against what he saw as a dangerous trend. "There is in this country a grossly exaggerated sense of what can be done by law, what can be done by ordering people around, what can be done by pieces of paper."[2] As he saw it, excessive regulation bred hostility among those who were on the receiving end of all of the rules, and created a political climate that made solving important problems all but impossible.

His warning, now four decades old, seems prescient today. In his remarks, Dunlop pointed out that in 1940 the Department of Labor had had 16 major statutes or executive orders to administer. By the time of his swearing in, that number had swelled to 134. Today, critics of regulation use much the same language that Dunlop did. The Mercatus Center, a libertarian think tank at George Mason University, found that the number of prescriptive words in the code of federal regulations—shall, must, may not, prohibited and required—mushroomed from 400,000 in 1970 to nearly 1,000,000 by 2008.[3] During the lead up to the 2016 presidential election, overregulation emerged as a key theme on the Republican side. As Democrats sought to call attention to income inequality as the cause of the nation's mounting economic anxiety, the GOP offered up a different explanation. Red tape was choking economic growth, and "the rising tide of labor regulations, health care mandates, tax codes and safety guidelines threaten[ed] to undermine America's entrepreneurial spirit."[4]

That message found a receptive audience. The populist backlash against elites that fueled Donald Trump's successful bid for the presidency was also a rejection of what Dunlop described as "ordering people around," and the technocratic elites responsible for those "pieces of paper." Trump's declaration at a presidential debate that he would roll back regulations while Hillary Clinton would increase them "all over the place" resonated with Republican voters, more than three quarters of whom said that government regulation is excessive.[5] And even as the new administration failed to make much progress on its legislative agenda during the president's first year, Trump quickly moved on his promise to cut red tape across government.[6]

Dunlop took office at the Department of Labor as a reformer, intent on doing his part to stem the rise of the 'third government,' the vast regulatory state of which he was officially part. And yet his critique of the dangers of regulation had little in common with today's crusaders against regulatory overreach. For one thing, Dunlop was as much a creature of the regulatory state as he was a critic. By the time he took the helm as secretary of labor, he'd spent much of his career moving between Harvard University and government service, including positions with the Wage Stabilization Division of the War Labor Board, the Office of Economic Stabilization, and most recently, the Cost of Living Council, where he'd been tasked with helping to unwind Nixon's wage and price control program.

But it wasn't just Dunlop's experiences working within—indeed, at the highest levels, of the regulatory state—that set him apart from today's critics of red tape. His cautions about the increasingly regulatory nature of the government originated from a very different place than, say, conservative and libertarian warnings regarding the encroachment of government upon individual liberties. Governing via regulation represented, from Dunlop's point of view, a failure to develop consensus and common views, which he regarded as absolutely essential to the workings of a democracy. Sixty years old when he accepted President Ford's invitation to lead the Department of Labor, Dunlop had spent his entire adult life getting warring parties to sit down and talk to one another, combining art and science to craft solutions to complex, seemingly intractable problems. "Out of conflict can come creative solutions that make both sides better off," Dunlop reflected in a sweeping 2002 interview about his career. "[T]he important thing is to express and channel conflict in ways that get the problems dealt with in a constructive manner."[7]

Relying on regulation, or worse, litigation, to solve problems meant giving up on efforts to convince and persuade, to develop consensus and mutual accommodation. But while Dunlop was critical of his era's overreliance on rules, law and "paper," he didn't see himself as anti-regulatory in the spirit of today's champions of deregulation. Rather he sought to revisit the methods of regulation, involving, to the greatest extent possible, the parties and people impacted by it. He also drew a sharp distinction between deregulation and what he thought of as regulatory reform: setting standards and enforcement procedures so as to arrive at a clearer understanding of the methods and processes of regulation. And unlike contemporary anti-government crusaders, with their deep aversion to labor unions, Dunlop believed deeply in collective bargaining as a mechanism for resolving disputes and facilitating what he thought of as constructive engagement. Rather than simply taking a hatchet to rules, Dunlop sought to redirect the role of government to improving understanding, persuasion, accommodation, mutual problem solving, and informal mediation."[8]

Dunlop arrived at the Department of Labor after a particularly intense time at Harvard. Like Columbia and the University of California's Berkeley campus, Harvard had been rocked by social unrest, reflecting tensions over the Vietnam War and civil rights. But as Dunlop well understood, the same divisions that had all but ripped Harvard apart were tearing at all kinds of institutions. In his inaugural remarks on that spring day in 1975, he worried aloud about the prospect of Americans retreating into "islands of self-interest." Dunlop implored the group that had gathered in his honor, symbolic, he noted, of the country's own diversity—"labor and management, academics and practitioners, old hands and young specialist, both sides of the legislative aisle, and active minority groups"—to build bridges, communicating agreement and disagreement alike. "Only then can we honestly solve the nation's problems."[9]

His tenure as secretary of labor, the highest-ranking government position Dunlop would hold during his lengthy career, lasted less than a year. In yet another parallel to the current era, Dunlop would fall prey to the Republican Party's increasingly vocal and organized right wing, which viewed organized labor as an enemy. While he would go on to serve presidents Carter and

Clinton, including chairing the latter's Commission on the Future of Worker-Management Relations, his largely behind-the-scenes roles have left him without the legacy of his contemporary and colleague George Shultz, for example. Within his academic work in the field of industrial relations, Dunlop was viewed as a pioneer. But here too, shifting tides, including the steady diminishment of labor unions in the US and the eclipse of the sort of "real world" economics in which he specialized, have diminished his legacy over time.

And yet Dunlop's approach to solving problems, applied over decades and across an impossibly diverse terrain of settings, has a unique applicability for today. Our contemporary era, with its condition of permanent political gridlock, partisan furor and gaping inequality, seems to abound in disputes beyond resolving, problems whose complexity bely solutions. To revisit a six-decade-long career devoted to what Dunlop would term "constructive" steps and solutions is to come away inspired anew by the possibility and promise of his work. Many of the particular challenges in which he immersed himself remain just as relevant now. Campus turmoil. Domestic manufacturing under siege from the forces of globalization. Spiraling health care costs. An undocumented immigrant workforce without labor rights or basic protections. Gaining insight into Dunlop's search for solutions and his construction of problem-solving "mechanisms" for these and other issues can help us think about the utility of his approach for the issues that confront us today.

WHAT WOULD DUNLOP DO?

What might Dunlop make of one of the most contentious issues of the present era, the battle over health care? Enacted by Congress without Republican support in 2009, the Affordable Care Act or Obamacare, remains hotly contested. The law, which was largely based on Republican ideas for health reform, succeeded in expanding health insurance to nearly 20 million Americans. But the debate over how—or even if—to provide insurance to Americans who otherwise would lack access to it remains as fractious as ever. At the core of the controversy is the perennial, and perennially unresolved, question of the role of government and how much or how little it should do. While Republicans have made the case for a minimal role, emphasizing what they see as the coercive aspects of Obamacare, the Democrats remain divided over the extent to which government's role should be further expanded. The uneasy stalemate that resulted from the collapse of Republican efforts to repeal and replace the law did nothing to bridge the vast partisan philosophical divide at the heart of the debate.

The complex, seemingly intractable nature of the health care fight makes it exactly the sort of issue that would have appealed to John Dunlop, argues health insurance expert Karen Ignagni, whom Dunlop mentored. "I think he would relish going to work in the current environment because he loved controversy. He loved opportunities to confront and deep and divergent philosophical divides."[10] Even the heated political rhetoric would have appealed to him, says Ignagni, who gave a talk at Harvard in 2016 on how Dunlop might approach the health care conundrum. "He loved situations where there was a lot of posturing and talking and very little listening because I think he thought he could get to work in those environments." Most of all says Ignagni, Dunlop relished the challenge of finding areas of compromise, no matter how elusive they seemed.[11]

In fact, in 1980, Dunlop led an effort to deal with the nation's emerging health care crisis, and the vexing combination of cost, access and quality. He brought together six national organizations all concerned with some aspect of the health care debate. Structured as one of the private labor/management committees that were among Dunlop's favorite problem-solving vehicles, the Group of Six, as it was known, consisted of the American Medical Association, the American Hospital Association, Blue Cross-Blue Shield, the Health Insurance Association of America, the Business Round Table, and the AFL-CIO. The group followed the basic pattern set by the Labor-Management Group that Dunlop had founded in 1973 as a government body, then ran as a private entity after stepping down as secretary of labor. Health care joined a long list of pressing public and political problems "for serious joint staff work on which consensus might be achieved."[12]

Ignagni first encountered Dunlop as part of this labor/management effort to confront the emerging health care crisis. For the AFL-CIO, where Ignagni was the Director of Employee Benefits, health care costs were rapidly emerging as a major issue; as costs ballooned, workers were being forced to accept cutbacks at the bargaining table. The challenge of trying to save worker benefits by transforming the way employees accessed health care intrigued Dunlop, who continued to work closely with the labor group long after he stepped down as secretary of labor. Ignagni would end up spending her entire career in the health insurance industry, serving as the CEO of America's Health Insurance Plan (AHIP), through which she was directly involved in the negotiations with the Obama Administration over the Affordable Care Act. Today she oversees EmblemHealth, one of the largest not-for-profit health plans in the US. Throughout her career, says Ignagni, her work with Dunlop and understanding of how he viewed the health care challenge has shaped her own approach to reforming the industry.

When Ignagni joined in the high-wire negotiations over the ACA beginning in 2009, she consciously tried to view the proceedings as her mentor might have. The first imperative: get to know the individuals involved, listen to them and find out where they come from. For Dunlop, listening was key. As he put it: "People don't always say what they fully mean and there is a therefore an art of learning to listen between the lines."[13] Those very first exchanges of information included essential background about the individuals on the other side of the negotiating table. That insight, says Ignagni, enabled Dunlop to begin to think about possible areas of compromise or ways that the sides might begin to work together. "How do you negotiate with the other side, what do both sides have in common, and how do you get from A to B?"[14]

"Nobody knew health care could be so complicated," remarked President Trump, with some exasperation, as his bold campaign plans to scrap Obamacare met the reality of the country's enormous, unwieldy health care system.[15] The Affordable Care Act had succeeded in expanding access to coverage to millions of Americans but had done little to address costs. And while soaring premium costs became fodder for campaign ads and talking points, no one was talking about how to address system-wide costs, what Ignagni describes as the aggregation of all of the costs in the system. That systemic view, including the costs that accumulate at every level—the charges by drug companies, hospitals and technology companies that get bundled into premiums—is the perspective from which Dunlop would have begun to approach the challenge, says Ignagni. "How do we think about a system that is consuming such a large part of our GDP in the country? How do we think about the sustainability of the system?"[16]

The word that is often used to describe Dunlop's approach to problem solving, "tripartite," refers to the three-way partnerships he facilitated throughout his career between labor unions and employers, the government acting as an "honest broker" between them. That the term has largely disappeared from common usage reflects the diminishment of labor's power and the end of the era of what Dunlop's colleague, Harvard economist John Kenneth Galbraith, called "countervailing power." With its complex overlap between public and private sector, however, health care remains uniquely suited to the sorts of collaborative relationships between government and the private sector in which Dunlop specialized, says Ignagni. During the lead up to and roll out of the Affordable Care Act, Ignagni, in her capacity as CEO of AHIP, essentially channeled her mentor. During the government's botched premier of the federal health care exchanges, and the urgent effort to fix them that drew together industry representatives, technology experts and government officials, Dunlop would serve as her essential guide. "[T]his was in effect a similar sort of process where people who came into a room had one objective, which was to solve a problem. We had to figure out how to develop trust, to keep confidentiality and to confront issues that were very, very messy."[17]

With the intense political acrimony that characterizes the present moment, defined by an inability of various actors to agree on basic facts, Dunlop's style of gathering together the various parties in the interest of finding common ground seems almost quaint. And yet Ignagni is convinced that that is precisely the approach he would have pursued. Again and again throughout his career, Dunlop would marshal key leaders around a common cause and a shared realization that cost of inaction outweighed the unpleasantness of trying to fix the problem. In this case, Ignagni surmises, Dunlop would likely summon the leaders of six key groups—the pharmaceutical companies, the unions, the employers, the health insurance plans, the hospitals and consumers—in order to tackle such issues as hospital consolidation and soaring pharmaceutical costs. "He'd say 'we have to hammer this out because it's our responsibility to take leadership to do it,'" says Ignagni.[18]

Regardless of the type or size of the problem Dunlop was attempting to solve, or the specific industry, he relied upon a similar set of techniques. Once the key stakeholders had been brought to the table, the ground rules lain, the real work began. Committee or staff groups, a favorite Dunlop vehicle, did the work of assembling information so that everyone at the table was looking at the same problem. "They didn't all agree," says Ignagni. "It's just like the Republicans and the Democrats. But everybody had to look at the data in the same way." That structure also had the effect of making problems seem more manageable. Stakeholders who had entered the room as sworn opponents found themselves conversing and exploring alternatives. "Not that they weren't arguing with one another about all sorts of issues, but there was that collegiality where there was a pathway to begin to solve problems," concludes Ignagni.[19]

NEGOTIATING CHANGE

With his strong ties to organized labor and a body of academic work largely focused upon industrial relations, Dunlop can appear as a creature of a bygone era. After all, the ranks of union members today are diminished to numbers not seen since the 1930's. But in the years following his departure from the Ford administration, Dunlop devoted much of his time to thinking about workers in industries that were being battered by globalization, or workers who lacked basic labor protections. In our current era, when unions are considered a relic, and "gig"-style employment is rapidly replacing traditional employer/employee relations, Dunlop's approach to helping workers remains an inspiration and a model.

Take, for example, Dunlop's resolution of a long-running dispute between the union representing migrant farmworkers and Campbell Soup, the subject of a chapter in this volume. The agreement that Dunlop helped hammer out resolved the dispute while providing a creative way to extend labor protections to a group of workers who lacked the protections of the National Labor Relations Act, making them especially vulnerable to abuse. The entity created to facilitate three-way dispute resolution between the farmworkers' union, the growers, and the big food companies that purchased their crops has evolved considerably in the 30 years since Dunlop traveled to the fields of northwestern Ohio to oversee union elections. Today the Dunlop Commission, as the entity came to be known, has expanded to include migrant workers in North Carolina, who travel to the US each year under the H-2A guest worker program. The agreement that covers these workers, based on the original agreement that Dunlop negotiated in Ohio, was the first to cover H-2A workers in the US.

As short-term employment increasingly replaces more permanent jobs, and the economy "fissures," with supply chains growing ever longer, the need for the sort of creative problem solving that Dunlop utilized to assist the farmworkers is more needed than ever, says David Weil, dean of the Heller School for Social Policy and Management at Brandeis University. Weil, who studied under Dunlop, collaborated with him on numerous projects, and took over for him as head of the Dunlop Commission in Ohio and North Carolina, points out that Dunlop viewed the absence of legal protections for workers not as an impediment to problem solving but as an opportunity. "The absence of a law here provided him with a 'blank canvas' with which to work out an entirely new mechanism to deal with problems facing farm workers," says Weil.[20] That mechanism required a union of farmworkers, an association of agricultural growers, and a new structure through which disputes could be resolved and grievances handled. Weil, the author of *The Fissured Workplace*, argues that in an era shaped by outsourcing and the resulting decline in wages, erosion of benefits and working conditions, existing labor law leaves out whole swathes of the workforce. "We need to modernize our regulations and laws, but we also have an opportunity here to think creatively about how to protect workers that our existing laws don't."[21]

Weil followed in his mentor's footsteps, leaving his post as an academic economist to run the Wage and Hour Division at the Department of Labor under the Obama administration. During his tenure, the Department of Labor issued a new rule, raising the salary limit that determined which workers were eligible for overtime pay. The rule change, years in the making, brought the salary threshold in line with where it would have been had it been indexed to inflation back in 1975, when the Dunlop Administration first established rules governing overtime eligibility. In 1975, more than 60 percent of salaried workers were eligible for overtime, a figure that had dwindled to around 7 percent by 2016, the result of inflation and changes enacted in 2004.[22]

Ironically, Dunlop pointed to the problem of trying to classify workers by salary level as evidence that the government had become both too regulatory and too detailed in its regulations. Referring to a decision to classify restaurant workers and fast-food workers differently for overtime purposes under the Fair Labor Standards Act, Dunlop warned that: "This sort of classification is bound to lead to endless litigation."[23] The 2015 rule changes, enacted by executive order without Congressional approval, were quickly attacked as an example of executive overreach. In 2016, the new overtime rule was invalidated by a Texas court after business groups and 21 states sued.

That the overtime salary threshold remained unchanged between 1975 and 2004, when it was updated by President George W. Bush, reflects, in part, the end of the brief era of cooperation between government, labor unions and industry of which Dunlop himself was so representative. When Dunlop left Washington in 1976 to return to Harvard after resigning as secretary of labor, he feared that he was leaving behind an administration in which there were no officials who understood labor unions or collective bargaining. The major projects he would embark upon following his "tour of duty," as he referred to his time spent in the Nixon and Ford administrations, were done outside of government for the most part. When he summoned forth leaders of industry and labor from the reaches of his extensive Rolodex, it was often to fill a void left by government's failure to act.

Jon Brock, who worked with Dunlop at the Cost of Living Council during the Nixon administration, and went on to help his mentor develop a dispute resolution mechanism for the public sector, is convinced that the view of Dunlop as a "tripartite" problem solver is inaccurate. "He got the parties to work together on a problem that government had punted," says Brock.[24] Still, government was never totally absent from Dunlop's work. Sometimes Dunlop's problem-solving mechanisms were loosely sponsored by government. Others received government sanction, giving them protection or the force of law, says Brock. He maintains that Dunlop's ability to craft solutions to complex problems that didn't rely entirely on government makes his techniques newly relevant for our current age. The Harvard professor whose first foray into problem-solving came at the behest of the Roosevelt Administration was an early adapter of the "work around" ethos flowing from Silicon Valley.

OVERVIEW OF THE BOOK

It would not be possible to capture a career as long and varied as Dunlop's in a single volume, and this book does not attempt to. Nor is what follows a biography. As he was fond of letting friends, colleagues and loved ones know, he had no interest in being the subject of one of these. Instead, this book explores the projects, problems and periods that Dunlop himself identified as being of key interest or importance. Each chapter is dedicated to a problem he set out to solve: the context, the "principals," and the problem-solving "mechanism" he set up. In each case, I've set out to convey the manner in which Dunlop saw the specific challenge or challenges that confronted him, and to capture his broader approach as well as the specific techniques that he deployed across sectors and settings.

Like Dunlop himself, the book moves between what he termed his "non-academic" stints, and Harvard University, where he was instrumental in defusing the explosive student revolt of 1969. Decades later, Dunlop would serve as Harvard's lead negotiator after clerical workers at the university formed a union. While he played some kind of policy role in virtually every presidential administration beginning in World War II, typically commuting between Cambridge or Belmont and Washington DC once a week, I've focused on the intense period of involvement that began with his appointment as the head of the Cost of Living Council in 1973. Tellingly, there is no neat chronological divide between the chapters. In fact, five of his most significant undertakings—President Clinton's Commission on the Future of Worker-Management Relations, a top-to-bottom reassessment of the US apparel industry, the establishment of a ground-breaking dispute resolution structure for undocumented farmworkers, a first contract for Harvard's employees, and the creation of the Joint Labor Management Commission for public sector dispute resolution in Massachusetts—all took place during the same time period.

While Dunlop produced an extensive, even enormous, body of academic work, there is far less to draw upon regarding what amounted to an entire other career in problem solving and dispute resolution. Beyond a few interviews he gave, including a sweeping retrospective conducted by economist Bruce Kaufman in 2002, and which I've drawn upon throughout this volume, Dunlop left little record of his non-academic work. Fortunately, a number of his former students, co-workers, academic colleagues and allies in the labor movement remain committed to keeping his legacy alive. I relied extensively on their recollections in order to reconstruct some of the key examples of Dunlop's approach to problem solving.

I am especially grateful to Dunlop's daughter, Beverly Donohue, who shared with me the personal diary that her father kept during the ten months that he served as secretary of labor. Started at the urging of *New York Times* editor and syndicated columnist Jimmy Reston, the diary chronicles Dunlop's time in office. Its pages provided me with an invaluable glimpse into how Dunlop thought about the specific challenges facing him, from a dispute over the shipment of American grain to Russia to the collapse of "situs picketing" legislation that would precipitate his departure, and his insistence upon using the opportunity before him to construct long-term solutions to short-term problems. He would dictate the diary entries on the weekends when he was back in Belmont with his family, his memory of events aided by his calendar and the notes he'd jotted down during an endless succession of meetings. The entries, on the original onion skin paper upon which his secretary at the time typed them, are full of references to characters who would go onto shape much of contemporary politics: Henry Kissinger, Don Rumsfeld, Dick Cheney, and a rising political star named Ronald Reagan.

Beyond affording a glimpse into the daily workings of government in the period following Nixon's dramatic departure from office, Dunlop's personal reflections captured the emergence of key trends, the importance of which we are only beginning to reckon with. There was the collapse of public faith in institutions, including the government. There was the growing resistance to regulation. There was the rise of the right wing of the Republican party, and the increasing influence of the business lobby over political debate and public discourse. Dunlop observed all of these with a sense of wariness. Solutions to the immense problems that confronted the country, from inflation, unemployment and the erosion of living standards to race relations, required that people talk to one another, and couldn't simply be imposed from above. They had to be negotiated—won through the hard work of persuasion, deliberation and changing minds.

NOTES

1. John T. Dunlop, personal diary, sec. 2, 3.
2. Diary, sec. 10, 26.
3. "Too Much Regulation Has Piled up in America," *The Economist*, March 2, 2017.
4. Matthew Shay, "Overregulation: Undermining America's Economic Engine," *The Hill*, May 3, 2016.
5. During both terms of George W. Bush's Presidency, the public was closely divided on the subject of regulation. After the election of President Obama, however, there was a dramatic rise in the number of Republicans who believed there was too much regulation. Gallup Governance Poll, September 7–11, 2016.
6. Danny Vinik, "Trump's War on Regulations is Real. But is it Working?" Politico, January 20, 2018.
7. Bruce Kaufman. "Reflections on Six Decades in Industrial Relations: An Interview with John Dunlop." *Industrial and Labor Relations Review*, 55, no. 2 (January 2002): 332.
8. John T. Dunlop, "Some Recollections of a Brief Tenure," *Monthly Labor Review*. 111, no 2 (February 1988): p. 46.
9. Diary, sec. 2, 3.
10. Karen Ignagni, interviewed by the author, March 25, 2016
11. Karen Ignagni, "The New Frontier of Health Policy and Delivery Reform: Can We Achieve it and How Would John Dunlop Guide Us." Lecture, the John T. Dunlop Memorial Forum, Harvard University, February 4th, 2016.
12. John T. Dunlop, *Dispute Resolution: Negotiation and Consensus Building* (Dover, MA: Auburn House Publishing, 1984), 254.
13. Diary, sec. 15, 36.
14. Ignagni interview.
15. Kevin Liptak, "Trump: 'Nobody knew health care could be so complicated,'" CNN, February 28. 2017. https://www.cnn.com/2017/02/27/politics/trump-health-care-complicated/index.html

16. Ignagni interview.
17. Ibid.
18. Ibid.
19. Ibid.
20. David Weil, interviewed by the author, May 4, 2016.
21. Ibid.
22. Steven Greenhouse, "Controversial Overtime Rules Take Effect," *The New York Times*, August 23, 2004.
23. Diary, sec. 5, 6.
24. Jon Brock, interviewed by the author, December 19, 2016.

Chapter One

The Harvard Wars

By the time Harvard University erupted in political furor during the spring of 1969, John T. Dunlop was one of the institution's most distinguished faculty members. Now into his third decade as an economics professor, Dunlop had authored key texts on labor and unions, the foundational *Industrial Relations Systems*, and had co-authored the seminal *Industrialism and Industrial Man.*[1] But his outsized reputation on campus owed as much to his high-profile role as a negotiator, mediator and problem solver as it did his lengthy curriculum vitae. Since 1943, when Dunlop had been asked by Franklin D. Roosevelt to join the War Labor Board as Director of Research and Statistics, he'd led what was essentially a parallel career outside of academia. Within his first six-months in Washington, he'd become, in his words, "a non-academic." While at Harvard, he taught, mentored, wrote and administered. Out in the world, however, Dunlop wrestled with complex real-world challenges: wage and price controls, inflationary spirals and wage-related labor disputes that threatened to cripple whole sectors of the economy.

"In a sense I have always regarded my Harvard and outside worlds as bifurcated," Dunlop would recall in a wide-ranging interview published in 2002.[2] His colleagues at Harvard mostly seem to have viewed his work the same way. The specifics of his work in Washington and with a wide array of labor organizations passed largely unknown on campus, save for among a small group of compatriots who shared his passion for labor economics, arbitration and policy. Dunlop's reputation as someone who knew how to broker agreements and "fix" things, however, extended to Harvard's highest reaches. As Roger Rosenblatt recounts in his memoir of the Harvard wars of 1969, Dunlop had been called upon the previous year when the campus had threatened to erupt over the invitation of Arthur Goldberg, a former labor secretary and Supreme Court justice with close ties to President Johnson, to speak on campus. Dunlop's strategy of engaging every conceivable interest group, and enlisting their responses and questions, paid off; Goldberg's talk went off without event.[3]

Dunlop would need all of his problem-solving savvy to rescue Harvard from the turmoil of the late 1960's. And while negotiating an end to, say, the nation-wide rail dispute of 1967, might seem a world away from calming Harvard's complex crisis, Dunlop relied upon the same tools he'd been honing for a lifetime. Negotiating, as he practiced it, was equal parts art and politics, requiring superior listening skills and a Machiavellian understanding of power dynamics, not to mention a bottomless supply of patience. Defusing the months-long crisis at Harvard involved first lowering the temperature on campus, then "working things out," as Dunlop put it, among various constituencies, including administrators, governing board members, students, faculty and community organizations. Within each were factions and divisions, reflecting a university, a community and a country, all deeply, deeply at odds over the Vietnam war.

But even as Dunlop sought to defuse the explosive tensions that wracked the university that he loved, he saw an opportunity to usher in lasting change to an institution that had long proven immune to it. The specific challenge at hand—negotiating an appropriate punishment for student protesters who'd been accused of violence—was also a chance to address long-standing problems at the famously decentralized school. Just as he'd done with countless labor disputes and policy dilemmas, Dunlop succeeded in creating an elegant problem-solving approach—what he thought of as a "mechanism"—to deal with Harvard's multiple and complex challenge in a constructive way.

CAMPUS CONFLICT

University administrators were expecting *something* to happen at Harvard. For months, student strikes and protests had upended campuses from the west coast—San Francisco State, San Fernando Valley State—to the east: Swarthmore College, City College of New York, Rutgers. Student activism at Harvard itself had been intensifying in recent years, growing increasingly confrontational. When Defense Secretary Robert McNamara came to campus to speak in 1966 but refused student demands that he debate an anti-war activist, some 800 students blocked his car, forcing him to escape through the university's network of underground tunnels. The next year, a recruiter visiting campus from Dow Chemical was held in a conference room of Mallinckrodt Hall by 350 students protesting Dow's involvement in the Vietnam war.[4]

As Rosenblatt recalls, the protest in front of University Hall on April 9 that would culminate in students seizing the building, wasn't even the first demonstration that day. In the early hours of that morning, a group of antiwar protesters and students from Students for a Democratic Society (SDS) had marched on the home of Harvard's president, Nathan Pusey. They massed in front of his Quincy-street residence, chanting "ROTC must go" and "smash ROTC," making their point by fixing their list of demands to Pusey's front door with a knife.[5]

At the University Hall demonstration, also led by SDS, some 300 protesters demanded of Harvard's leaders what they'd been urging for months: that Harvard end its involvement in the Vietnam War, specifically its contracts with the Reserve Officer Training Corp or ROTC. This time, though, the students went beyond their typical marching and chanting, or even the symbolic knife planted in the president's door. Swarming the steps of University Hall, they took their case directly to the men who ran Harvard, demanding that the deans leave their offices or be thrown out.[6]

If university administrators were on high alert, they didn't give any indication on this particular day. As the protesters moved through University Hall and its administrative offices, they found most of Harvard's deans within, working at their desks. Fred Glimp, dean of Harvard College, was there. So too were the deans of the Faculty of Arts and Sciences, the Graduate School of Arts and Sciences, the Dean of Students, along with the Dean of Freshmen, F. Skiddy von Stade and his assistant dean, Archie Epps. Mostly the "transition" of power, as students told Harvard's leaders to clear out of their offices, was peaceful. But a handful of administrators got rougher treatment at the hands of the occupiers. Dean of Students Robert Watson was dragged through the halls, while Archie Epps, the sole African American administrator on Harvard's leadership team which, as Rosenblatt notes, made him the target of particular derision by the protestors, was pushed down a flight of stairs before being forcibly ejected from the building.[7]

Once they'd kicked out the building's official occupants, more than 100 students set up camp in the deans' offices and the Faculty Room. "Mainly the atmosphere was fun," Michael Kazin recounts to Rosenblatt. One of the three co-chairs of SDS, Kazin explains that despite the circus-like atmosphere in University Hall, the occupiers were deadly serious. "We did not aim simply to desecrate the temple. We were fighting a war to stop a war."[8] As the occupiers made clear in their first official statement, they intended to remain in University Hall until the Harvard Corporation ceded to their demands:

> We are holding University Hall to force the Harvard Corporation to yield to our demands. We intend to stay until we win. These demands are nonnegotiable, and for very good reasons. For instance, we consider the ROTC as a life-and-death issue for the people of the world whose lands are occupied by U.S. troops, whose social revolutions are fought viciously by the U.S. military.[9]

The occupation would last less than 24 hours. At dawn on April 10, Harvard's gates, locked since the previous afternoon, were reopened, allowing hundreds of police officers from Cambridge and surrounding communities to swarm Harvard Yard. The police worked quickly and methodically, clearing the Yard of protesters and pursuing some students into nearby Thayer Hall. Using a battering ram, the police broke down the doors of University Hall, ejecting the occupiers with far more force than the students had used on the previous day. The bust was quick, lasting about 15 minutes, and violent—more than 75 students would end up in local hospitals or at the University Health Services. Some 250 students were arrested, many sent to Cambridge City Jail, where they would be charged with trespassing.[10]

By 6AM, the police officers were gone, but they left behind a deeply divided campus. President Pusey himself had approved the use of force against Harvard's own students, acting on the advice of law professor Archie Cox, who, having been part of a committee that studied the Columbia University riots of 1968, recommended a policy of "fast bust or no bust."[11] Conservative faculty quickly lined up behind Pusey and his get-tough approach, while their more liberal counterparts were horrified by the police action, even as they disapproved of the behavior of the student occupiers. While the occupation and the university's response brought into sharp relief long-festering divisions among Harvard's faculty, among students the events played the opposite role. Students had never been united behind SDS and its goals, but the police bust coupled with frustration at President Pusey's unwillingness to listen to student demands knit them together. "He was pretty dogmatic in response to challenges to authority," John Dunlop would later say of Pusey.[12]

Dunlop was one of the faculty members who was deeply disturbed by the Pusey administration's response to the occupation of University Hall. "He thought it was really deplorable, and in many ways it was," recalls Derek Bok, who was then the dean of Harvard Law School, and would go on to serve as Harvard's president for two decades. "I think it was the single worst year in Harvard's history in terms of a response to an outside problem. The faculty was totally demoralized and didn't know how to function."[13] A distinguished economics professor who'd arrived at Harvard in 1938 as a teaching fellow, the 55-year-old Dunlop was by then something of a legend on campus for his negotiating prowess and problem-solving abilities. But as Dunlop would confess to Bok over lunch at the Faculty Club days after the police bust, the problems confronting the university seemed of a magnitude beyond the sorts of labor/management disputes that he was forever being called upon to untangle.

While Bok and Dunlop were long-time colleagues and collaborators, even friends, Harvard itself was a subject they never discussed. That day was different, recalls Bok. "This was the first time that John had really talked to me about the university and its problems." That the subject of Harvard had never come up between them before was itself a sign of just how Balkanized the university was, says Bok. Housed in two different schools, on different parts of the campus, his and Dunlop's common world was labor relations, not the university where both had spent decades. As they sat together in the dining room of the Harvard Faculty Club talking about the turmoil unfolding around them, Dunlop only became more exercised, recalls Bok. "I remember John at one point bringing his fist down hard on the dining room table and saying 'I'm going to do one of two things. I'm going to get the hell out of this institution or I'm going to turn my attention to it full-time and fix it.'"[14]

THE COMMITTEE OF FIFTEEN

Dunlop's attempt to "fix" the institution began with the Committee of Fifteen, a special faculty/student committee formed in response to the student occupation and its aftermath. The committee, officially voted into existence at a contentious faculty meeting just days after the police bust, was tasked with looking into what had happened on April 9th in order to determine how Harvard should respond. At the heart of the new committee's business was the question of how—if at all—the student occupiers should be punished. While the faculty had voted to dismiss all of the charges against the students, a Cambridge judge had ruled that students who'd been charged with criminal trespass had to stand trial, regardless of what Harvard itself determined should be their fate. To the many divisions laid bare during that spring of 1969, here was another one: town vs. gown.

But the business of the Committee of Fifteen went well beyond the discipline question. In addition to writing up a history of the events, the group was tasked with making recommendations regarding Harvard's future governance. Rosenblatt, who served as a junior faculty representative on the committee, notes that the group's importance was evident in its mission. "[I]t represented the wresting of power from the administration. In a way, it was the faculty's direct and formal statement of contempt."[15]

The Committee of Fifteen was officially elected into being by Harvard's faculty on April 17th. The group included seven tenured faculty members: John Dunlop, James Q. Wilson, Alan Heimert, Milton Katz, John Edsall, Stanley Hoffman, Gerald Holton and Benjamin Schwartz, along with two non-tenured faculty representatives: Donald Anderson and Rosenblatt. Five students would also be included: Keith MacAdam, John Read, John Fernandez, Renée Chotiner and Robert Blumenthal. The delicate balance of liberal and conservative faculty, along with the decision to include students, was the product of intense behind-the-scenes negotiating—and the deft hand of John

Dunlop. In fact, the very structure of the group bore his imprint; it had been set up to function as what Bok describes as a "problem-solving mechanism."

The committee's mission was to be carried out through an elaborate network of subcommittees, a regular feature of Dunlop's style of problem-solving. But as Rosenblatt recounts, the division of labor did more than merely facilitate the committee's work. It also served to keep separate the group's three-part focus. Disciplining the students, ostensibly the most important, not to mention explosive, task before the committee, was divided from the recommendations for changes to Harvard's governance structure, which was to remain distinct from the investigation into the causes of Harvard's unrest. Writes Rosenblatt:

> As long as the history of the causes was kept apart from the recommendation for structural change, and those two assignments were kept apart from the disciplinary decisions, it would be impossible to confuse finding fault with the University with the punishment of the students. That is, if the committee yoked its several functions under one report, the disapproval of the bust or conceivably the opposition to the war could serve as an extenuating circumstance for shoving a dean down the University Hall steps. Whatever was wrong with Harvard, as with America, was kept as a separate issue from the behavior of the people in the occupation.[16]

Even the process for selecting the students to serve on the committee hints at a mechanism at work behind the scenes. The faculty had settled on a balance of 10 faculty members and five students. One student, Keith MacAdam, was elected as the representative of Harvard's graduate students, while Renée Chotiner, then a junior at Radcliffe, was elected to hold the designated "Cliffy" spot. The remaining three students were to be selected from Harvard's undergraduate houses. But because there were ten of these, an additional step was added to the selection process.

"There were ten of us and we were all paraded over to Widener Library," recalls John Read, who was in the running as the designated representative of Eliot House.[17] The group was ushered into the book-lined sanctum of library director Merle Fainsod—a sort of library within the library, says Read. A hat was proffered up and ten marbles appeared, one for each house. The three students who drew green marbles—the remainder were red—had a spot on the committee. Read, who was then a senior at Harvard and about to become a father for the first time, was one of the chosen three.

John Fernandez was another of these. If Read's path to Widener that day was a well-trodden one—his brothers, father and both grandfathers had all attended Harvard—Fernandez' was far less likely. The sole African-American member of the Committee of Fifteen, Fernandez was the first in his large Cape Verdean family to attend college—just one of his four sisters had finished high school. He'd transferred to Harvard from Northeastern

University, but only after spending four years in Turkey and Morocco as part of a naval security unit. When the head of Dudley House encouraged him to apply for the Committee of Fifteen, Fernandez, by his own admission, knew almost no one at Harvard. With two young children and a full-time job, he was rarely on campus. But Fernandez, who was a member of the Black Panther Party, was a forceful speaker, a skill that propelled him past the other student candidates for the post. Still, when it came time to draw his marble, he asked the president of his house to do it for him. "I didn't feel lucky," recalls Fernandez.[18]

The Committee officially convened on April 18th at Eliot House, less than 10 days after the student occupation. As Rosenblatt recounts, Dunlop made straight for the disciplinary committee. "John Dunlop saw clearly from the start that the disciplining of the students was the only thing that really mattered."[19] Students involved in previous campus incidents, including the surrounding of Defense Secretary McNamara's car and the "hostage taking" of the Dow Chemical representative, had been disciplined by the university. This time, however, the charges were more serious, the division over what should happen to the student protestors far more profound. That division, which cleaved students from administrators, and liberal faculty from their conservative counterparts, was also represented within the ranks of the committee.

On the one side were the "law and order" faculty members, whose ranks included James Q. Wilson and Dunlop himself, and who were pushing for the maximum punishment for the student offenders. On the other were more liberal faculty and the student representatives who sided with the occupiers. John Fernandez, for example, viewed the occupation as an entirely legitimate form of protest. "They didn't hurt anyone," recalls Fernandez. "The university wasn't responding to their demands. Ten percent of my high school class got killed in Vietnam, so I had strong feelings about this."[20]

But while Wilson was clearly a hawk—Fernandez remembers him as a "right-wing fascist"—Dunlop's precise views are harder to discern. Rosenblatt, for example, maintains that Dunlop approached the committee's work with a clear vision in mind: "Throw out the student radicals and you'll show everyone who is in charge; that is what he understood."[21] But student member John Read argues that Dunlop was up to something far more subtle. By laying out the expulsion of the student protesters as the starting point, Dunlop spurred the students towards compromise, says Read. "I'm convinced to this day that he purposely set the bar out there so that these young punks could feel like they were making progress and come to consensus."[22]

Dunlop also played the role of peacemaker when conflict would erupt between the more radical students and the "law and order" voices, which included Harvard's lawyer, Archibald Cox. Fernandez recalls one incident when Cox argued that the student protestors should be thrown out. "They weren't poor like you," Cox said to Fernandez. Dunlop, likely sensing trouble, stepped in to try to smooth things over. "He said 'let's not play on this class divide because Fernandez doesn't buy that stuff.' I think he figured out early that he needed me and John Read on his side," says Fernandez.[23]

MEETINGS, MEETINGS

The committee would meet for a total of five weeks, much of that time devoted to elaborately choreographed "hearings." Each day, the subcommittee members—Dunlop, Wilson, Katz, Rosenblatt, Fernandez and Read—would assemble in the "courtroom" on the tenth floor of Holyoke Center, Harvard's main administrative building, to hear the testimony of the deans, and the 155 students who'd been implicated in the occupation and in the "manhandling" of Dean Epps and others. Except that the students, who refused to recognize the legitimacy of the tribunal, didn't show. When they did appear, recalls Fernandez, it was to protest the proceedings, their presence seemingly terrifying the faculty members. "One day all of these militants came to Holyoke Center and all of the professors were panicking. They wanted to call the police," recalls Fernandez. But Dunlop, no doubt realizing the incendiary elements at play, had another idea. He suggested that the two "strong young men" on the committee, meaning Fernandez and Read, were all the security that the group needed. "They can handle whoever comes to the door," Dunlop said.[24]

As the discipline committee attempted to assemble a factual record of what precisely had happened on April 9, another subcommittee set to work drafting a resolution intended to codify rules for future protests at Harvard. The history and governance subcommittees were also meeting regularly, and periodically the entire Committee of Fifteen would reconvene. "We met and we met again, and again," writes Rosenblatt. "[I]n the mornings, in the afternoons, in the evenings."[25] The meetings lasted for hours, recalls Fernandez, the assorted members debating, among other things, what did and did not constitute violence. "It would be 11:00 at night and most people would just want to go home and that's when you'd hear John Dunlop say 'I have a solution that might work here,' or 'I have a possible compromise,'" says Fernandez. "He'd wear you down."[26]

The Committee of Fifteen wasn't alone in its constant meetings. The liberal and conservative faculty caucuses, formed in the immediate aftermath of the occupation, were also convening seemingly every day, conducting long, heated meetings in which they debated both student and administration complaints. Here too Dunlop would play a key role, including shaping how the meetings were run. As a guard against the tendency of key faculty members to pontificate endlessly, overwhelming the kind of focused exchanges that Dunlop believed were so key, he imposed a limit on faculty speaking time. He even procured an oversized hourglass, and, as each speaker took the floor, audience members could watch for themselves as three minutes of sand passed through the glass' narrow neck.[27]

While Dunlop's sympathies lay with the conservative block, his mechanism for pushing towards consensus and resolution entailed organizing the more sensible, pragmatic people within that grouping, recalls Derek Bok. Dunlop had an elaborate system for organizing faculty within the meetings, says Bok:

> If he saw something that was put on the agenda or brought up for a vote, he would give a kind of signal. He had three or four lieutenants who would fan out and round up all of the people who were on John's team of 'acceptable people.' They would leave their offices and hustle over to the meeting in time for the vote. John didn't lose many votes. The other side wasn't nearly as organized as he was.[28]

The most contentious of the faculty votes was the one to establish a department of Afro-American Studies, and have it in place, including the chair, by the start of the following semester. The vote, which came in response to demands from Black students at Harvard, established an unusual committee made up of faculty and students tasked with shaping the new department. The vote reflected the faculty's extreme wariness of provoking another student uprising. In the days after the police bust, a student strike had been called, but was called off after the faculty voted to restrict the activities of ROTC on campus. As Rosenblatt notes, the vote on the new African-American studies had the effect of giving a group of Harvard students more power than junior faculty like him who had no say over department tenure decisions.[29]

The decision to give Black students an outsized say in the creation and running of the new department effectively sowed the seeds of its demise.[30] But the faculty vote was also a response to the glaring reality that Harvard's faculty was both pale and male. In 1969, Harvard had a single tenured woman on its faculty, recalls Bok. And she was only there because Radcliffe had established a professorship that had to be held by a woman. Dunlop would become a tireless recruiter of women and minorities, utilizing the ad hoc committee process established by the faculty during that tumultuous spring. "John was an extraordinary recruiter," says Bok. "He saw that the university was way behind the times."[31]

VERDICT REACHED

As April gave way to May, the end of the school year looming ever nearer, the Committee of Fifteen's work was at last nearing completion. And yet on campus, the group's verdict on what disciplinary consequences the students should face remained a contentious mystery. Would the committee determine that the radicals should be thrown out, as Archibald Cox and James Q. Wilson had called for publicly? Or would they heed the demands of Harvard's students, some 2,000 of whom had signed a petition arguing that "no one should be severed or suspended from Harvard due to their actions at University Hall"?

As the students pointed out, expelling students could mean sending them to Vietnam as they would be eligible for the draft. Meanwhile, as the "gowns" continued to mull over the students' fate, the "town" had already delivered its verdict. Cambridge judge Edward Viola found that 170 students of the original 174 were guilty of criminal trespass, sentencing one of them, Carl Offner, to a year in prison for allegedly shoving Robert Watson, Dean of Students.[32] Even as debate raged on campus, the committee members continued their deliberate process of determining what precisely had happened on April 9th. John Read recalls that the focus on facts had the effect of lowering the temperature in the committee meetings. "It became clear during the process that the sentencing was going to be much more mild," says Read.[33]

Ultimately the Committee of Fifteen didn't recommend that any students be permanently expelled from Harvard. Sixteen of the 135 students who had been in University Hall were asked to leave. The three who'd been found to have physically assaulted the deans were recommended for "dismissal" from Harvard, meaning that they could only be readmitted with a two-thirds vote of the faculty. A handful of students who'd been involved in damaging property during the occupation were "separated" from the university for a period of one or two years, while the remainder were "admonished" for their actions.

All of these were recommendations, however. The Committee of Fifteen, constituted by the faculty less than two months earlier, had no ability to act but could only present its findings to the faculty and recommend a course of action. On June 9th, the faculty convened at the Loeb Drama Center, among the few venues on campus large enough to accommodate the gathering. Dunlop himself spoke on the reasoning behind the committee's disciplinary determinations. James Q. Wilson elaborated on the specific actions being recommended against individual students. Rosenblatt presented on the Resolution on Rights and Responsibilities, the passage of which was necessary in order to legitimize the committee's recommendations. But the starring role, the job of presenting the committee's findings to the Faculty of Arts and Science, went to a student: John Read.

The idea was Dunlop's, naturally—the "mechanism" at work. "It was a masterful bit of theater on John's part," says Read. Making a student the voice and the face of the Committee of Fifteen sent a powerful signal to the larger Harvard community: that the deep divisions that had seemed to threaten the very institution weren't so intractable after all. Says Read: "In a very serious sense, that, coupled with the two-year-long governance committee process was what allowed the tensions on the campus to ease."[34]

TOUGH LOVE

The findings and recommendations of the Committee of Fifteen took the form of a 77-page interim report, distributed to the entire Harvard community, including incoming freshmen, who received the document in the mail prior to their arrival on campus. As the *Harvard Crimson* noted, the document described the college in "less than bucolic terms." In addition to the report on the investigation into the causes of the crisis, the report on disciplinary decisions and the Resolution on Rights and Responsibilities, the pamphlet also included a brief, final section hinting at deep structural changes required at Harvard: The Plans of Working Group Three. The explosive issue of disciplining the student occupiers had been defused, but the task of fixing what was wrong with Harvard itself was just beginning.

The governance committee process that followed the Committee of Fifteen's work would never attract the same level of attention as its predecessor but it would succeed in transforming the way that Harvard was managed. Here too Dunlop would play a key role. Recalls Derek Bok: "John recognized that this wasn't just a narrow problem of how we responded to radical students and minority student demands. He saw this as a symptom of fundamental problems in a university that hadn't adapted to changes in the world and was ill-equipped to deal with the future."[35]

Dunlop would become Dean of the Faculty of Arts and Sciences in 1970. And while the specific questions of governance and university leadership differed from those that his discipline subcommittee had spent weeks mulling over, Dunlop's style of work—his problem-solving mechanism—remained much the same. There was the tireless behind-the-scenes maneuvering and the out-organizing of his opposition, not to mention his legendary ability to outlast almost anyone, foe or friend, at a meeting table. Then there was the immense body of knowledge about Harvard that Dunlop had somehow accumulated. Bok, who became president of Harvard in 1971, said that he was awed by the wealth of detail Dunlop had at his disposal. "He knew about the strengths and weaknesses of every department," says Bok. "It was really quite amazing. John never liked to be in a situation in which he wasn't very well informed, better informed than anyone else."[36]

Bok credits Dunlop with ushering Harvard through its most difficult chapter, and with helping evolve a management structure equipped to handle the demands of an enormous, complicated institution. Within a few years, the insular presidency of Nathan Pusey and his predecessors had been replaced by Bok, who was a modern style of executive, while a raft of vice presidents and provosts greatly expanded the management team. While the battles between the conservative and liberal faculty caucuses raged on, a new faculty council ensured that faculty members had more voice in decision making. Progress was even made on diversifying Harvard's overwhelmingly white, male faculty, due in no small part to Dunlop's tireless recruitment efforts.

"The person who held us together and got us through wasn't me at all," Bok recalls. "It was John. He managed to push the university into a much better outcome. It was a remarkable, really a remarkable job."[37]

A COMPLEX SITUATION

In his sweeping retrospective interview with Bruce Kauffman, Dunlop included the great student/faculty rebellion at Harvard as one of the most complex situations he'd ever been called upon to help resolve. The array of moving parts, the deep internal divisions within the university, the political factions, even the challenge of long-winded professors threatening to overwhelm faculty meetings, all made a resolution seem unlikely, if not impossible. If resolving conflicts in labor-management relations often entailed a "family of disputes," here was an entire campus of them.

While the conflict proved uniquely challenging, the tools and skills that Dunlop utilized in order to help Harvard heal, and, more importantly, set the institution on a more stable course for the future, were ones he would draw upon regularly during his decades as a problem solver. The understanding that out of conflict and tension can come creative solutions that leave everyone better off; the ability to identify opportunity amidst turmoil; even the strategic use of autonomous committees as part of a larger problem-solving mechanism—these elements provide the essence of the Dunlopian approach to dispute resolution. To tackle his next real-world challenge, unwinding wage and price controls at the Nixon-era Cost of Living Council, Dunlop would utilize many of the same strategies he'd relied upon during that long season of struggle at Harvard University.

NOTES

1. Dunlop co-authored the 1960 volume with Clark Kerr, Frederick Harbison and Charles Myers.

2. Bruce E. Kaufman, "Reflections on Six Decades in Industrial Relations: An Interview with John Dunlop." *ILR Review* 55, no. 2 (January 2002): 328.

3. Roger Rosenblatt, *Coming Apart: A Memoir of the Harvard Wars of 1969*, (Boston: Little, Brown, 1997) 113.
4. Jean E. Engelmayer and Melissa I. Weissberg, "Reflecting on the 1969 Student Strike," *Harvard Crimson*, April 9, 1984.
5. Roger Rosenblatt, 30.
6. William Galeota and William Kutik, "Students Occupy University Hall, Eject Deans, Staff, from Offices," *Harvard Crimson*, April 9, 1969.
7. Rosenblatt, 11.
8. Rosenblatt, 16.
9. Ibid.
10. Justin Lerer, "Yard Watches Students Seize University Hall," *Harvard Crimson*, June 3, 1977.
11. Rosenblatt, 14.
12. Engelmayer and Weissberg, 1984.
13. Derek Bok, interviewed by the author, May 5, 2016.
14. Ibid.
15. Rosenblatt, 61.
16. Rosenblatt, 108.
17. John Read, interviewed by the author, September 7, 2016.
18. John Fernandez, interviewed by the author, September 13, 2016.
19. Rosenblatt, 108–109.
20. Fernandez interview.
21. Rosenblatt, 109.
22. Read interview.
23. Fernandez interview.
24. Ibid.
25. Rosenblatt, 118.
26. Fernandez interview.
27. Beverly Donahue, email correspondence with the author, May 7, 2017.
28. Bok interview.
29. Rosenblatt, 141.
30. The faculty eliminated the special role of students in 1973 during Dunlop's tenure as Dean of the Faculty of Arts and Sciences.
31. Bok interview.
32. "Offner's Sentence," *Harvard Crimson*, May 19, 1969.
33. Read interview.
34. Ibid.
35. Bok interview.
36. Ibid.
37. Need note.

Chapter Two

Out of Control

In January 1973, John Dunlop departed Harvard for another of his "non-academic" stints in Washington, DC, this time to head up the Nixon Administration's Cost of Living Council. He'd spent a full five years immersed in the business of Harvard University, including serving as one of its top administrators. A *Harvard Crimson* profile that ran on the eve of his departure for Washington captured the university's "most colorful and freewheeling figure" in action at a faculty meeting. "Dunlop slouches in his chair," observed the writer, "scowls disdainfully in the direction of his ever diminishing number of adversaries, only to jerk upright in paroxysms of laughter when his side scores a point."[1]

But while his adversaries may have been dwindling, his friends weren't growing in number either. As Dunlop would explain to Derek Bok, who had recently become Harvard's president, the five years he'd spent pulling Harvard back from the brink and putting it back together had come at a steep cost: he'd lost his love for the place. Recalls Bok: "He said 'you cannot function effectively as a dean unless you really love the faculty and students, and the events that we've been through have left me with so many people who I basically despise, that I can't really be an effective dean.'"[2]

Dunlop's diminished affection for the institution he called home wasn't the only reason that he was eager to depart for Washington. The complex challenge of unwinding President Nixon's wage and price controls was exactly the sort of real-world problem solving that Dunlop relished. In August of 1971, President Nixon had announced a new economic policy targeting unemployment, inflation and international speculation. Wages and prices were to be frozen for 90 days—the first such controls during peacetime in US history. Nixon also announced the creation of a new Cost of Living Council (CLC), tasked with figuring out how to stabilize wages and prices after the temporary controls were lifted. Phase 1 marked the sudden imposition of controls, Phase II an effort to make them more flexible.

Dunlop would take the helm of the CLC in time for Phase III: the delicate and confounding process of trying to wean the economy off of wage and price controls. While he had been considering Nixon's offer of the directorship of the CLC since the previous year, he didn't formally accept until the administration rolled out the third phase of the new economic plan. "My guess is that he could have involved himself any way he wanted to in the past," Bok told the *Harvard Crimson*. "I don't think that Phase II offered the same opportunities to work at the problems he's interested in." [3]

Dunlop's departure for Washington came on the heels of a particularly intense period in the academic part of his life. Unofficial "fixer" of the university as Harvard descended into the turmoil of the late 1960's, Dunlop had officially become Dean of the Faculty of Arts and Sciences in the summer of 1970, a title that brought with it plenty of new responsibilities. In addition to trying to hold together a deeply fragmented faculty, Dean Dunlop oversaw the nuts and the bolts of the university: 40 departmental and institutional budgets, recruitment goals, even setting tuition and room and board fees for the following year.[4] It was perhaps a sign, however, of how he'd come to view Harvard, with its student protests and constant inter-faculty warfare that the Nixon administration's effort to unwind wage and price controls in a time of economic turmoil appeared as something of a respite. As Dunlop put it, here was a chance to "get back to his profession": industrial relations.[5]

When Dunlop penned a new introduction in 1992 to his classic volume, *Industrial Relations Systems*, which first appeared in 1958, he paid tribute to a generation of economists and lawyers for whom the Great Depression and the reforms of the New Deal had served as a kind of real-world apprenticeship. He was both inspired by this tradition and placed himself squarely within it:

> I perceived the facts of wages, labor markets, labor organization, management and government roles as well as conflict resolution from an academic background, but no less from the crucible of practical decision making as mediator, arbitrator, academic officer in training, or government official, where the consequences of perceptions and judgments are 'swift and sometimes terrible.'[6]

Dunlop was lamenting the rise of a new generation of academics, labor economists in particular, who had never worked in government, and rarely encounter anyone else who had either. The result was a far narrower vision of the world than the one held by Dunlop and his predecessors—industrial relations pioneers like John R. Commons, the University of Wisconsin labor historian, or Harvard's Sumner Slichter. "Their judgments about the real world are untested," Dunlop wrote of this new generation. This was far more than a mere curmudgeonly rant. In a provocative article penned after his time at the CLC, Dunlop reflected that academic analysis and effective policy making was separated by "vast distances—as if they were in millions of light years."[7] Indeed, he went so far as to argue that contemporary analytic work by academic economists and labor relations specialists was essentially useless. "These academic activities in my experience are almost totally irrelevant to the major problems confronting decision makers in government, and in labor and management as well, and, in fact, they have had almost no influence on actual decisions."[8] By leaving Harvard for Washington, he was also siding with the "practical men" over the "men of philosophical temperament," as Alfred North White described them in a quote that Dunlop cited regularly.[9]

Dunlop was granted two years of leave from his position as Lamont University Professor, the distinguished professorship he'd held at Harvard since 1971, but he would need less than half of that. Phase III would survive just six months; Nixon's experiment with direct economic controls, including the CLC reached its end in the summer of 1974. Indeed, even as Dunlop prepared to assume his new post, the warning signs regarding the immensity and complexity of the task he'd signed on for were unmistakable. For one thing, there seemed to be a great deal of confusion about what precisely Phase III *was*.

Nixon officially announced the beginning of Phase III on January 11, 1973. Effective immediately, the wage and price controls of the previous 17 months, with the exception of food, healthcare and construction, were officially over. Gone too were the Pay Board and the Price Commission. The president called instead for what he termed "voluntary cooperation" by labor unions and corporations, which he expected to continue to adhere to the standards that had been in force in an effort to keep down inflation. And to ensure compliance from unions and companies, especially large ones, Nixon held out the threat of renewed government wage and price regulation. Whereas Phase I had meant the sudden imposition of a wage-price freeze, and Phase II wage and price "standards" aimed at overcoming the inflationary wage/price spiral, Phase III ushered in the era of "self administration" of the regulations.[10] But the new voluntary policy also meant lost leverage as the tool of offering companies early exit in exchange for commitments on wages and prices was off the table.

What precisely did "voluntary cooperation" and "self administration" mean? Not even Nixon's own officials seemed to agree. The job of wading into the policy weeds and explaining the inner workings of Phase III to the country fell to Nixon's new Secretary of the Treasury, George Shultz. A highly-regarded economist from the University of Chicago, Shultz served as Nixon's labor secretary prior to becoming the chief economic official in the administration. But despite the fact that Shultz and Dunlop were both labor arbitrators—both had been regular attendees of Sumner Slichter's seminar at MIT—there were important differences between the longtime friends and colleagues. If Dunlop saw the role of government as a broker between workers and companies, Shultz was a proponent of free market solutions, including to the country's current economic woes.

"The basic thing is competition—the free market. That is the fundamental force we rely on over a period of time to keep things under control," Shultz explained in an interview.[11] His preference for a free market fix was on vivid display during a press conference explaining the details of Phase III. As William "Bill" Walker, who was the General Counsel to the Cost of Living Council, recounts in his history of the period, Shultz gave the clear impression that the government was backing away from the wage and price controls that had been in effect since Nixon's 1971 announcement.

"While [Shultz] said that the Administration retained the authority to reimpose mandatory controls in sectors where inflation threatened to get out of hand, his clear message, which the journalists duly communicated to the American people, was that controls were lifted and prices were free to rise,"[12] writes Walker. The next day, the *New York Times* broadcast the sudden change in policy with a front-page story, complete with a dramatic—and oversized—headline: MANDATORY WAGE-PRICE CONTROLS ENDED EXCEPT IN FOOD, HEALTH AND BUILDING FIELDS; NIXON CALLS FOR VOLUNTARY COMPLIANCE. The proclamation of Phase III, observed *New York Time*s reporter Edward Cowan, who would chronicle the administration's economic policies throughout their evolution, "was nearly as startling as his announcement of Phase I."[13] The stock market responded accordingly. On January 11, the very day that Nixon named Dunlop as the new head of the CLC, the market plunged, marking the start of the worst downturn since the Great Depression.

CHANGING COURSE

If Phase III was off to an inauspicious start, the leadership transition at the CLC was somewhat rocky as well. In taking the helm, Dunlop was replacing Donald Rumsfeld, who was leaving to become the US Ambassador to NATO.[14] Charismatic and gregarious, Rumsfeld presided over a tight knit staff of young men who were intensely loyal to him. Bill Walker was one of these. Walker had followed Rumsfeld to Washington from Evanston, IL, where he'd chaired Rumsfeld's re-election campaign to Congress. He recalls the transition from Rumsfeld to Dunlop as traumatic. "Don's departure to NATO was upsetting and changed the chemistry significantly," says Walker.[15]

That the culture of the CLC was about to undergo a serious change was obvious during the literal changing of the guard. At a going away party for Rumsfeld, staffers performed a song meant to make light of the occasion, complete with lyrics: "Will they perform for the John as they did for the Don?" Dunlop was not amused, recalls Walker.[16] He used the occasion to deliver a brief, stern lecture about the challenges of ending wage and price controls once they'd been imposed, and how he viewed Phase III as an opportunity to learn from past mistakes and try out new ideas. While Walker knew of Dunlop by what he describes as his "gruff reputation," it was his first up-close sighting—and the start of somewhat tense relationship, at least initially. "I had a very rough go with John during Phase III because I was the one who had to say no to his ideas," says Walker.[17]

While Dunlop took pride in his "real world" academic training, reserving special disdain for academic economists he regarded as hopelessly "Ivory tower," the reality was that his approach to the thorny problems he was now tasked with untangling was far more academic than that of his predecessor. Cowan, the *New York Times* reporter, lamented that his questions about policy were now met with, well, an economics seminar. In a story on Phase III written just after Dunlop replaced Rumsfeld, Cowan described asking a question about mandatory price controls and food and receiving "a reply about the law of supply and demand and the Government's recent and forthcoming measures to expand farm output."[18]

But others delighted in Dunlop's insistence on bringing a bit of the flavor Harvard to Capitol Hill. When, for example, it came time to deliver special testimony to a Congressional oversight committee, Dunlop saw it as an opportunity to introduce committee members to fundamental economic concepts. Recalls Hank Perritt, who served as the executive secretary for the CLC: Dunlop wanted to explain "how economists hadn't predicted the run up to inflation and how difficult it was to enforce wage and price controls in such a complex economy."[19] Perritt was tasked by Dunlop with preparing the lesson for the oversight committee, and then sitting alongside his boss at the witness table. "It was a wonderful experience," recalls Perritt, who likens his time at the CLC under Dunlop's leadership as "like being a precocious seminar student."[20]

Dunlop would extend the seminar approach to other aspects of his work at the CLC, defining his role there as not just a director but a teacher. Once a week, Dunlop and assorted staffers would meet with key members of the Washington press corps, including print journalists for the top dailies and news magazines, as well as network newscasters. "The elite of the press would come for an economics session because of John," recalls CLC Deputy Director Jamie McLane.[21] For an hour, Dunlop would hold court, explaining how the economy actually worked, complete with charts demonstrating, for example, the process by which commodities move from a farm to the consumer's hands. Or, starting with a widget, he might explain how raw materials, wages and production determined the price of an automobile. But as McLane notes, Dunlop's "teaching" role here played a purpose beyond just presiding over an economics seminar for journalists. The larger goal was to convince the press corps that wage and price controls *didn't* work. "What we were trying to do was point out all of the bad things that wage and price controls did," recalls McLane.[22]

To that end, Dunlop and his crew had plenty of real-world examples to point to. As Phase II gave way to Phase III, inflation soared. The combination of the Federal Reserve's expansive monetary policy and years of pent up demand meant intense pressure on supply, resulting in shortages and sending commodity prices skyrocketing. Oil prices were the first to rise, as oil companies took advantage of Phase III's more relaxed approach to price hikes and did just that. Then there was the dramatic increase in food prices. In the first quarter of 1973, the cost of food rose at a staggering rate, with consumer food prices increasing by nearly 30 percent, and red meat prices rising by 90 percent.[23] The CLC responded by re-imposing price controls on commodity prices, a measure that caused a near revolt among farmers.

Dunlop had only to point to the headlines, about tomato farmers dumping their product in downtown Little Rock, to demonstrate the failures of wage and price controls. Or more vividly still, he could bring as a visual aid to one of his weekly economics "seminars" a crate of the chickens that were arriving from chicken farmers, who calculated that it would be cheaper to send them to Capitol Hill than to raise them. Such real-world examples helped Dunlop and his staff explain how inflationary bubbles form but also served a larger, unarticulated purpose: to put to rest the enabling legislation that had allowed for the use of direct economic controls in the first place. Recalls McLane: "Our real hidden goal was to ensure that the enabling legislation wasn't reenacted when it came up. We were one of the few agencies in the government, I think, whose goal was to put itself out of business."[24]

PHASE IV

But even as Dunlop and the Council were making the case against wage and price controls, calls for the administration to do *something* were rising along with inflation. President Nixon, one eye on his slumping poll numbers, another on the ever-encroaching Watergate investigation, took action.[25] On June 13, 1973, Nixon delivered a nationwide TV address to announce the imposition of another round of price freezes. While Nixon's decision went against the advice of Dunlop and Shultz, the President also used his speech to convey his strong distaste for economic controls, which he likened to an addictive drug. "If our economy is to remain dynamic, we must never slip into the temptation of imagining that in the long run, controls can substitute for a free economy or permit us to escape the need for discipline in fiscal and monetary policy," said Nixon. "We must not let controls become a narcotic; we must not become addicted."[26]

The price freeze was to be temporary, lasting sixty days, during which the CLC was to come up with some new means of fighting inflation. Once the sixty-day period was over, Phase IV would commence, to be characterized by some new set of controls, designed by the CLC, to finally help wean the economy off of its control "habit." In many ways the task before the CLC was far more daunting than in the first days of Nixon's New Economic Policy. Yet for Dunlop, it was a challenge that he relished. When he'd arrived in Washington to take over from Rumsfeld, he'd joined an operation already well under way. What was more, the transition from academia back to public service hadn't been seamless.

Take the issue of public vs. private deliberation. In his 1990 volume, *The Management of Labor Unions*, Dunlop drew contrasts between the four fields of business, government, academia and unions. One key difference between academic and government "processes," he noted, was that while the former were largely private with periodic exposure, the process of government was necessarily public at each step. But he bridled at the insistence that everything in government needed to be done "under the full blast of publicity and in public." [27] Serious negotiations, as he was fond of pointing out, never took place in public, as the spotlight favored speechmaking over constructive conversation, and made pragmatic changes in positions all but impossible.[28]

"One can go too far either in the way of secrecy or in the direction of openness, which precludes and hamstrings effective action," Dunlop would reflect in his personal journal the following year, but his style of work in Washington—indeed, wherever he was—seemed to favor a behind-closed-doors approach over public scrutiny.[29] Back at Harvard, if he had an issue he needed to resolve he could simply summon the relevant parties to a meeting. The same was true of the business and union leaders with whom he carried out the work of the Construction Industry Stabilization Committee. He had only to pick up the phone or issue a summons for them to join him, whenever, wherever. But government didn't operate that way. "The major issue I have," complained one unnamed source to the *New York Times*' Cowan, "is that [Dunlop] doesn't distinguish between private arbitrage and public business."[30]

Walker recalls a car ride with Dunlop during which he had to explain to him the U.S. statute on open meetings. "I told him 'you can't just have private meetings.' He was furious with me," says Walker. "He practically threw me out of the car. He didn't like the bureaucracy and the process by which government had to conduct its business."[31]

A TEAM OF TIGERS

When asked if he was enjoying his job as director of the CLC, Dunlop responded that the question was "outside my frame of reference. I'm the son of a Calvinist missionary."[32] The quote appears in a profile of Dunlop that ran in the *New York Times* in October, 1973, the work of Edward Cowan, the economics writer whose job it was to cover the daily developments on the wage-price beat.[33] Cowan interviewed Dunlop at a cocktail lounge and includes in the story their negotiation over where to sit.

Cowan: Where do you want to sit?

Dunlop: Any place that's dark and in the corner.

Cowan: Why don't you take the banquette?

Dunlop: With my back to the wall, as usual?[34]

The writer is clearly enamored of the professor, whom he describes as "vital, curious, didactic and combative." Writes Cowan: "[Dunlop] brings to real-world problems the precision of scholarly analysis and the practical cunning that knows when to opt for ambiguity." As an aside, Cowan praised Dunlop for his being an efficient administrator, noting that "his staff likes him."[35]

"Here's the deal," Walker recalls Dunlop telling his team after returning from a White House briefing on the latest price freeze.[36] And they *were* his team now. The choppy waters of the Rumsfeld transition were officially in the past, and Dunlop now commanded the loyalty of his predecessor's deputies: Bert Conlan, Walker, McLane, Perritt and others. He'd also brought in his own staffers to round out the group, including John Read, the Harvard student who'd since graduated from Harvard Business School, and who had played such a key role on the Committee of Fifteen. They were, as Perritt describes, "a small group of tigers: smart, quick and quite young."[37] The days were long and everybody worked hard, nobody harder than Dunlop himself. He'd be in his office hours before the start of the official work day, thinking, while his meetings with business and labor leaders over drinks or dinner at a Washington DC watering hole, ran late into the night.

Yet somehow even with the nonstop economic emergencies, the committee meetings and the Congressional testimony, Dunlop also found time to mentor his young charges. To Hank Perritt, who had come aboard the CLC under Rumsfeld at just 26 years of age, Dunlop was like a beloved professor. Dunlop would grant his deputy, Jamie McLane, an "honorary doctorate" when their time at the CLC was up. "He knew I'd almost failed economics at Yale, but he blamed that on Yale. At the end of it all, he said 'you know more than all of my PhD students after going through this,'" recalls McLane.[38] For John Read, the chance to work as Dunlop's executive assistant was the continuation and deepening of a mentorship that had started during his senior year at Harvard.

In the personal diary he would keep during his next stint in Washington, as Secretary of Labor, Dunlop reflected that mentoring his young staffers was key to developing their loyalty and attachment. And he paid close attention to their larger career goals and how the time spent working alongside and under him might further those. Dunlop's opinions on this matter were quite firm: a person shouldn't be recruited for a job unless it made sense to their development and trajectory, "toward some further objective which that individual highly regarded."[39]

While wrestling with hyperinflation and commodity shortages was a challenge of a different order than holding together the Harvard faculty or determining the disciplinary consequences for student protesters, Dunlop's approach to solving these real-world economic problems featured some familiar elements. He quickly enacted his favored committee structure: establishing advisory committees with considerable autonomy. "You set them up and let them go; you don't try to control them," says McLane. "Let them come back with their recommendations and thoughts. You don't have to agree with them but you get a different perspective."[40]

To the elaborate organization hierarchy of the Economic Stabilization Program with its offices of economic policy, productivity, price stabilization and congressional affairs, Dunlop added largely independent bodies headed by industry leaders representing key sectors of the economy: food, healthcare and construction. The committee structure reflected Dunlop's view that the economy wasn't a monolith but rather was comprised of sectors, some of which were recovering while others continued to decline. Essentially, these largely independent bodies also allowed Dunlop to bypass the bureaucratic workings of government and its emissaries, with which he was so impatient, in favor of the industry leaders who actually had the power and the inclination to do something about the problems that the CLC was tasked with fixing.

Take Earl Butz, the secretary of agriculture, whose name appeared on the official CLC Committee on Food. Butz was fond of reminding Dunlop that he bore no responsibility for food prices, recalls McLane. "It's not the food that's expensive, it's the plates and the silverware you eat it with," Butz would often say.[41] Meanwhile, the Food Industry Advisory Committee, led by Don Perkins, the CEO of the Jewell supermarket chain in the midwest, was where Dunlop went when he needed information or advice about the sector. Perkins, who'd started his journey through Jewell's corporate ranks as the driver of a delivery truck in California, was an inexhaustible source of knowledge, which he was more than happy to share. "[Dunlop] spent a lot of time talking to Don," says McLane.[42]

Meanwhile, Dunlop devoted much of his time and energy to the area in which he was most knowledgeable: the construction industry. The Construction Industry Stabilization Committee, which Dunlop had headed since 1971, was now led by his Harvard colleague Quinn Mills. But Dunlop continued to play an active role, convinced that reducing the size of wage settlements, which tended to have a domino effect across the construction industry, was key to solving the wage side of inflation. Just as he had used the information he'd managed to acquire regarding Harvard and its many departments and institutes to help knit a fractured university back together, here he relied upon his knowledge of wage rates among different unions in different parts of the country to keep wage settlements down.

BATTLE OF THE BULGE

Even as Nixon's sixty-day price freeze remained in effect, Dunlop issued a strong public warning that there were likely to be significant price increases once Phase IV was officially implemented. As Dunlop explained to *New York Times* reporter Edward Cowan, "The notion that prices should be expected to be stable after the freeze—agriculture or non-agriculture—seems to me not an accurate reflection of underlying facts."[43] The reason for this was what Dunlop referred to as a "price bulge." Business costs had been rising faster than prices, meaning that when the freeze ended there was likely to be a "bulge" of higher prices.

Dunlop was insistent, however, that the price increases on the corporate end, all of which had been approved by the CLC, were justified. The infamous "stick in the closet" that Shultz had alluded to at the start of Phase III had remained there. Said Dunlop: "There were no widespread violations." Cowan reported that Dunlop delivered the words with 'some feeling' "There was no occasion to pull a stick out of the closet and hit somebody for violating the law." Dunlop's strong words, wrote Cowan, were meant as firm retort to persistent critics of Phase III's 'lack of teeth,' and who wanted a return to a more aggressive form of wage and price controls.[44]

But even as Dunlop was warning the country to prepare for a bumpy road of higher prices ahead, the "tigers" at the CLC were grappling with the complex task before them. As Walker writes in his memoir of the period, Phase IV's general approach, as outlined in a CLC staff paper, consisted of "limit[ing] the speed and size of the pass-through of cost increases and to take all available steps to increase supply and reduce the prices of important inputs in the food and industrial sectors."[45] On the supply side, that meant, say, increasing farm acreage. On the price side, companies were going to be on the hook for increasing costs. Phase IV, notes Walker, represented a transition "from the freeze to the squeeze."[46]

As Dunlop explained to the press corps, the challenge facing the planners at the CLC was "how to manage the Phase IV bulge, how to spread it out." Elsewhere he would describe the American economy as resembling a snake that had swallowed a tennis ball. It was up to him and his team to figure out how to reduce the size of the obstruction and spread it out over time. 'Spreading out the bulge' meant releasing different sectors of the economy at different times so as to spread the price increases out. In pursuing this strategy, Dunlop finally had the opportunity to treat the economy sector by sector. He could also exercise leverage, either in fact or in perception, over what sector leaders would need to do in order to be liberated from controls. Working with leaders of individual sectors, Dunlop and his colleagues determined what was needed in order to insure longer term stability. They would then "call the parties to Washington and cut a deal that would free them from control," recalls Read.[47]

The task of decontrolling the economy sector by sector was made infinitely more difficult by the lack of up-to-date industry-wide data. As Read recalls, Dunlop used the leverage of lifting controls to convince industry leaders and a trade association group to work together to create a database to assist with further stabilization. Access to adequate and accurate data was far from the only challenge Dunlop and his colleagues faced, however. All through the spring and summer of 1973, commodity prices continued their dramatic rise. Farmers, who were infuriated by the freeze, began withholding crops and livestock from the market. By August 1973, meat shortages had broken out across the country, while severe soybean shortages resulted in the imposition of an export embargo, disrupting international trade.

But the most dramatic increases were in petroleum prices, the result of a complex confluence of factors far beyond US borders. Crude oil prices had been rising steadily since 1970, as US production declined and global demand soared. Under Phase IV, the price of crude oil was capped, with steady increases planned through the end of the program. It made sense, at least on paper, but when the OPEC nations announced in October of 1973 that they were doubling the cost of a barrel of oil, the result was a huge spread between the controlled cost of oil and what suppliers were now demanding.

If the petroleum problem was particularly confounding, it was representative of the larger challenge confronting the CLC. Again and again the planners' efforts were disrupted by unforeseen events, often unfolding far from the US, that would then ripple through the supply chain. Then there was the political drama that had suddenly erupted in Washington. October 20, 1973, the date of the OPEC oil increase, was also the Saturday Night Massacre that began when Nixon demanded that Attorney General Elliot Richardson fire Watergate Special Prosecutor Archibald Cox, Dunlop's long-time Harvard colleague. Richardson refused, as did Deputy Attorney General William Ruckelshaus, until Solicitor General Robert Bork ultimately fired Cox. The nonstop news stories about rising prices finally had some competition: Watergate.

WINDING DOWN

Within six months, the nation's experiment with wage and price controls would be over. The CLC succeeded in realizing what McLane insists had long been its real mandate: putting itself out of business by making sure that the enabling legislation that made controls possible wasn't re-enacted. Dunlop's mission of communicating to the press all of the harmful consequences of wage and price controls had also been realized, while the public increasingly shared Dunlop's opinion as the once popular measures came to be associated with shortages and price hikes. By the time Dunlop appeared before the Senate Banking Committee in 1974 for hearings on the Economic Stabilization Act, wage and price controls had few defenders left. Ultimately, Congress let the Act expire signaling the official end to both the "freeze" and the "squeeze."

While Dunlop and the CLC staffers wrapped up their operation, the Watergate scandal bloomed all around. In March of 1974, George Shultz would step down from his post as the secretary of the treasury. McLane announced his own resignation the very next day. "I knew that if [Shultz] resigned, something was going on. Watergate was beginning to bubble up more."[48] Dunlop, recalls McLane, was understanding but urged his deputy to stay on the job a little longer. "He said 'I'd like you to help me wind this down.'"[49] McLane relented and stayed on the job until June 30, when the CLC officially ceased operations for good.

The other "tigers" moved on as well. Perritt was tapped to head up the official CLC wind up operation under the Secretary of the Treasury. He would later move to the White House to join Don Rumsfeld in the chief of staff's office of the Ford Administration. Bill Walker would move to the Department of Energy, serving as general counsel, before joining the Ford Administration as the Director of the Presidential Personnel Office. John Read, meanwhile, headed back to Massachusetts in order to work for the governor.

During the intense period of Dunlop's time at the CLC, he would often wrap up the day over dinner with one of his staffers. Jamie McLane recalls one of these evenings: a late-night meal after yet another twelve-hour day of hearings, briefings and committee meetings. McLane complained to his boss about what he regarded as the unbearable politics of Washington DC. "I said to him: 'Between the White House and the Congress, it's just awful. I don't see how anything gets done.'" Dunlop found this amusing, says McLane. He leaned across the table, eyes crinkling with a wry grin and, with his trademark rasp, said: "the politics of Washington is nothing compared to the politics of Harvard University."[50]

Dunlop was returning to Harvard, his plans for the near future uncertain. He didn't expect the transition to be particularly difficult, Dunlop told the *Harvard Crimson*, because he'd been commuting home to Belmont every weekend since accepting the CLC post.[51] As a University Professor, Dunlop was free to teach in any department. The only option he ruled out without hesitancy was another administrative post. After an intense period in Washington immersed in the complex business of wage and price control policy, Dunlop would also return to his academic discipline, armed with a heightened conviction that his sectoral understanding of applied economics was correct, and more impatient than ever with the "millions of light years" that separated analytic economics from the policy decisions he'd been making.

In his challenge to academic economists, written in 1977, Dunlop laid out what he described as the principal tasks of policy makers, both private and public. They were: "to build their institutions, to change them through policies and personnel to confront new challenges, to develop an internal consensus, to build viable relationships with allies, and on occasion to engage in rivalry and conflict. A sense of opportunity, timing, and the art of problem solving is decisive." It's an apt description of his time at the CLC and the challenges of Phase IV: freeing the economy from wage and price controls one sector at a time.

NOTES

1. Daniel Swanson, "Good-Bye John: An Adversary Departs," *Harvard Crimson*, June 14, 1973.
2. Derek Bok, interviewed by the author, May 5, 2016.
3. Bok, cited in Swanson, 1973.
4. Arthur Lubow, "Dunlop Resigns to Take Nixon Post," *Harvard Crimson*, January 11, 1973.
5. Beverly Dunlop, email correspondence with the author, May 7, 2017.
6. John T. Dunlop, *Industrial Relations Systems*, (Boston: Harvard Business School Press, 1993), 3.
7. ———, "Policy Decisions and Research in Economic and Industrial Relations," *Industrial and Labor Relations Review*, 30, no. 3, (April, 1977): 275.
8. Ibid., 276.
9. Dunlop notes that he'd begun his 1944 volume, *Wage Determination Under Trade Unions*, with the Whitehead quote, "which is even more germane today." Dunlop, Industrial Relations Review, 1977, p. 282.
10. Edward Cowan, "Mandatory Wage Price Controls Ended Except In Food, Health, Building Fields; Nixon Calls for Voluntary Compliance," *New York Times*, January 12, 1973.
11. Edward Cowan, "Raising Prices Appears Easier," *New York Times*, January 27, 1973.
12. William N. Walker, "Forty Years After the Freeze," unpublished manuscript, November 2011.
13. Cowan, "Mandatory Wage-Price Controls Ended," *New York Times*, January 12, 1973.

14. According to Hank Perritt, who served as the executive secretary to the CLC, Rumsfeld had gotten a "whiff of Watergate" and was eager to distance himself from the Nixon Administration. Interview, January 18, 2016.
15. William Walker, interviewed by the author, October 7, 2016.
16. Ibid.
17. Ibid.
18. Cowan, January 27, 1973.
19. Hank Perritt, interviewed by the author, January 18, 2016.
20. Ibid.
21. Jamie McLane, interviewed by the author, May 17, 2016.
22. Ibid.
23. Walker, 12.
24. McLane interview.
25. Walker speculates that Nixon's decision to override his economic advisors was the work of senior adviser Melvin Laird, who convinced Nixon to re-impose price controls as a "show of political muscle."
26. Richard Nixon, "Address to the Nation Announcing Price Control Measures," June 13, 1973.
27. John Dunlop, *The Management of Labor Unions,* (Lexington, MA, Lexington Books, 1990), 13.
28. John Dunlop, personal diary, section 8, 2.
29. Ibid, 4.
30. Edward Cowan, "Wage-Price Missionary," *New York Times*, October 7, 1973.
31. Walker interview.
32. Cowan, October 7, 1973.
33. Dunlop notes in his personal diary that his relationship with Cowan had started off "on not too friendly terms." By the end of his stint as Secretary of Labor, however, a genuine friendship seems to have developed. "I think it is fair to say that our relationship is now excellent," Dunlop wrote. Diary, Sec. 18, 14.
34. Ibid.
35. Edward Cowan, "Wage-Price Missionary," *New York Times*, October 7, 1973.
36. Walker interview.
37. Perritt interview.
38. McLane interview.
39. Diary, Sec. 18, insert A.
40. McLane interview.
41. Ibid.
42. Ibid.
43. Edward Cowan, "Dunlop Sees Significant Rise in Phase IV Prices," *The New York Times*, July 13, 1973.
44. Ibid.
45. Walker, 16.
46. Ibid.
47. John Read, interviewed by the author, September 7, 2016.
48. McLane interview.
49. Ibid.
50. Ibid.
51. Mark Penn, "John Dunlop Will Return to Harvard When Washington Post Ends," *Harvard Crimson*, June 10, 1974.

Chapter Three

Tour of Duty

When Dunlop accepted Nixon's invitation to head up the Cost of Living Council, he'd gone to Washington as a reformer, intent on helping free the economy from an addiction to damaging wage and price controls. In 1975, he joined the Ford Administration as the secretary of labor. The appointment offered yet another of the "non-academic" adventures Dunlop relished, and at the highest level of service he would ever attain. But the cabinet position also provided him with the opportunity to press for reform. For the previous three decades, Dunlop had served one presidential administration after another, resolving disputes, overseeing wage-price stabilization programs, and leading a commission on work rules. His long service and unique perspective left Dunlop feeling increasingly concerned, even worried, about the encroachment of government regulation that he believed was essentially choking off the persuasion, conversation and negotiation that he believed were so key to meaningful problem solving. As secretary of labor, Dunlop hoped to use his position to push back against this trend.

Putting his reformer's ethos to work during his "tour of duty," as Dunlop would refer to his time as secretary of labor, also meant going beyond addressing the surfeit of short-term problems he inherited with the position. Again and again, Dunlop sought to create more permanent solutions, and embed problem-solving mechanisms, within the Department of Labor and beyond. When he arrived in Washington in the spring of 1975, Dunlop had no idea how long he'd be staying; he planned on making the most of this opportunity.

A WARM WELCOME

"Rarely has any Cabinet officer been sworn in during as gala and heavily attended a session as was [John] Dunlop on March 18," wrote syndicated labor columnist Victor Riesel in 1975.[1] The ceremony itself took place in the East Room of the White House and was attended by the heads of seemingly every labor union in the country, along with AFL-CIO chief George Meany. The festivities would continue the next night at a private dinner in Dunlop's honor held at the F Street Club near the White House. Some 50 labor leaders and government officials gathered at the behest of three previous labor secretaries: Arthur Goldberg, Willard Wirtz and George Shultz. These "party rounds" signified labor's deep satisfaction with Dunlop's appointment, wrote Riesel. "They're all with him—all the way from Meany to Fitzsimmons—with no intermediate stops or complaints," wrote Riesel of the labor leaders. "Most of them are on a first name basis with the man from Harvard. He knows them and the practices, needs and demands, as Billy Graham knows the bible."[2]

For the unions, especially those representing building trades workers, President Ford's selection of Dunlop represented the first time they'd had one of their own in the influential position of secretary of labor. The more recent candidates had been held in decidedly mixed regard by the working men they supposedly represented. While George Shultz shared Dunlop's background in mediation, the unions never considered him an honorary member like they did his academic colleague. Peter Brennan, the labor secretary whom Dunlop was replacing, came from the New York City building trades but had fallen out with George Meany early in his tenure over the pace of minimum wage hikes. As a result, the powerful AFL-CIO chief refused to utter Brennan's name in public, and he was noticeably absent from the ceremonies welcoming Dunlop back to Washington.

What accounted for the unions' devotion to a Harvard professor of economics who'd never actually belonged to a trade union? As Dunlop noted in his 2002 interview with labor historian Bruce Kaufman, he'd gained an invaluable first-hand understanding of poor employment conditions in the 1930's through the lives and stories of the migratory laborers that he and his brother hired to work on the family pear ranch in Eldorado County, California.[3] If that experience and perspective had helped to set Dunlop's particular trajectory in motion, it was his connections with labor leaders that would solidify it. In 1942, Dunlop helped his colleague Sumner Slichter set up the Harvard Trade Union Program to give union leaders the same kind of training that Harvard Business School provided to management. Dunlop, who taught in the program every year, says that it afforded him the opportunity to "develop close contacts with a whole series of labor leaders in all kinds of industries."[4]

Dunlop's work in wage stabilization and dispute resolution, including his recent stint overseeing the Construction Industry Stabilization Committee, also brought him into close contact with all kinds of labor leaders. In the 2002 interview, a sweeping retrospective that Dunlop gave at the age of 88, he estimated that he had mediated more than 50 national agreements between international unions. "You get to know these people, gain access to them, and develop working relationships," Dunlop reflected. "I suppose it is fair to say that at one time or another I have known the president of nearly every national union in the building trades, in transportation, and many of the industrial unions."[5] At least some of these relationships developed into close personal ties, as was the case with the AFL-CIO's George Meany. In fact, as Dunlop held court at his regular DC hangout, the Old Rogues Bar, the union leaders who joined him as he sought to untangle one thorny problem after another, were also his friends.

While the union leaders Dunlop had taught and consulted with over the years regarded him as "one of their own," they never lost sight of the fact that he was an academic. Indeed, it was his renowned ability to function in all three realms—the university, government and labor—that they most appreciated about him. It wasn't just that he understood "their" issues. The same could certainly be said about Brennan, who'd begun his own career as a union painter. It was Dunlop's ability to communicate the issues and concerns so paramount to labor leaders to government officials that they most appreciated. As one anonymous "high labor chap" put it to Victor Riesel: "When that bunch in the White House [Economic Policy Board Executive Committee] meet with John, they will understand what the world is all about. That's the biggest thing to us about Dunlop."[6]

BACK IN THE CABINET

When President Ford went searching for a labor secretary, Dunlop was an obvious choice. While other names were floated about, including Bill Usery, head of the Federal Mediation and Conciliatory Service, Dunlop had a powerful set of friends and associates rooting for him. Donald Rumsfeld, whom Dunlop had replaced at the Cost of Living Council, was now serving as Ford's chief of staff, and George Shultz, now the head of the Bechtel Corporation, remained an influential voice. Dunlop's advocates appear to have made a convincing case on his behalf. In his official remarks at Dunlop's swearing in on March 18, 1975, Ford welcomed the Harvard professor into the cabinet, paying tribute to his unique skills in "obtaining practical solutions to the most complex of problems."[7]

The president went on to mention a few of these problems. Jobs were at the top of the list; Ford let it be known that he was relying on Dunlop for "sound, practical programs" that would produce these quickly. The president also made mention of Dunlop's problem-solving skills and ability to break through the most difficult disputes. "John, we need you in the Department of Labor. We need the genius that made you the head of the economics department at Harvard University," Ford said, welcoming his new cabinet member. "We need you to obtain voluntary restraint without guidelines."[8]

Left unmentioned in Ford's welcoming remarks was the electoral politics problem that the President was hoping his new secretary of labor could help solve, specifically luring the building trades unions with which Dunlop had such close ties into the Republican voting column.

Ford was seeking to continue and expand upon efforts made by the Nixon administration to woo conservative union members. Nixon had appeared well on his way to winning key labor support in his 1972 bid for re-election, but backlash within the construction unions over the administration's imposition of wage controls and suspension of the Davis-Bacon Act on federal and federally-assisted construction projects had caused the coalition to unravel. On the eve of another election, the votes of building trades workers who were increasingly embittered over such issues as rising taxes, school busing and what they saw as the preferential treatment of Black workers and women, seemed to be up for grabs, and Ford believed Dunlop could help deliver them.

Dunlop, meanwhile, chose to use his swearing in to address more weighty matters than was typical for a largely symbolic occasion, as he recalls in the personal diary that he would keep throughout his ten months in office. He critiqued the present-day political climate that privileged a short-term policy focus above the longer-term interest of the country and cautioned about the dangers of overregulation, a tendency "peculiarly evident" in the very department he was poised to lead. Dunlop rattled off a series of alarming statistics. In 1940, the Labor Department had 16 major statutes or executive orders to enforce. By 1960 that number had risen to 40, and by 1975, to 134.[9]

Dunlop's insistence upon infusing a ceremonial event with seriousness would quickly become a theme for the new secretary of labor. As he saw it, adding substance to an occasion like his swearing in was a way of ensuring that the job itself was substantive. Of course, using a six-minute speech to introduce important research, international comparisons or concise explanations of how inflation worked wasn't easy, Dunlop conceded. It took time, not to mention staffers who understood that even brief remarks or presentations represented an opportunity to influence people's thinking, "or at least stimulate them to reflect upon substantive questions."[10]

PRIORITIES AND PRINCIPLES

On a Sunday afternoon in April, Dunlop adjourned to the study of his Belmont home for a few hours. He was back in Boston for the weekend, a custom he'd hold to throughout his time in the cabinet, and was taking advantage of the late day quiet to dictate his journal: a voice record of recent meetings and events, as well as his observations about the political and economic challenges of the times. Dunlop had been encouraged to chronicle his time as secretary of labor by *New York Times* editor and syndicated columnist Jimmy Reston. The diary was a first for Dunlop—he notes that he'd never succeeded in keeping one before, and that doing so would require "more of a disciplinary order of my life than has been conventional in that past." But taking a few minutes here and there to "jot down ideas and reflections as well as an account of events that may be of more general and future interest," seemed well worth it, Dunlop noted. These new experiences were of such interest to him that he didn't want to forget them.[11]

Despite his initial doubts, Dunlop quickly fell into a routine for recording new diary entries. Using his schedule of the previous weeks' meetings and appointments to jog his memory, he would craft as complete an account as he could, being careful not to allow too much time to elapse, less events become "a matter of ancient memory."[12] The tapes would then be presented to his long-time secretary, Helen Knox, for transcription. On this particular Sunday, he revisited the previous week's cabinet meeting at which Henry Kissinger had spoken at length on the latest developments in South Vietnam and Cambodia, and what he saw as a real lack of authority in the US in dealing with the rest of the world. Ford had called on Dunlop towards the meeting's conclusion to say a few words about the method for dealing with the press that he'd developed while working at the CLC and had restarted at the Department of Labor at the request of the reporters themselves.

In the five minutes allotted him, Dunlop had quickly explained the rationale for his approach to working with the press and gave cabinet members a sampling of recent sessions: the structure of unemployment and how unemployment was calculated, the operation of the unemployment insurance system, and an explanation of the current economic outlook that encouraged reporters to understand the economy as being comprised of multiple sectors in varying states of health. While Dunlop conceded that his own academic and professorial background made this approach easier for him to carry off than it might be for others, he encouraged cabinet members—indeed anyone working at the federal level of national leadership—to consider working with and educating the press as part of their jobs. When Ford asked Dunlop what happened if the journalists in his course failed to learn the lesson, Dunlop responded that it might be appropriate to take them elsewhere for what he termed informal consultation. "The whole matter was played on a very light plane on my part."[13]

TOUR OF DUTY

Dunlop had spent his time at the CLC the previous year trying to unwind the Nixon administration's wage and price controls even as inflation spiked. And while President's Ford early declaration that he wouldn't request Congressional authority to use such controls meant that Dunlop and his team had succeeded in making the case against them, inflation raged on. By the time Dunlop took the helm at the Department of Labor, the economy, which had been in recession for months, was in the midst of a sudden sharp downturn. Unemployment surged and economic output plunged, even as prices continued to rise at alarming rates. Meanwhile, the fear of further igniting inflation meant that policy makers were seriously constrained regarding what they could do to try to fight it. Ford's conservative economic advisors sounded a steady drumbeat against what they warned were the inevitable inflationary pressures of deficit spending. But even a relative moderate like Dunlop worried that federal spending would lead to a decrease in much-needed private sector investment at the plant and industry level.

The combination of forces confirmed his growing sense that the Keynesian project itself had run out of steam. As Dunlop lamented in his diary: "We live in an economic world at present where government expansionist policies through fiscal measures do not necessarily lead to economic growth."[14] He used the analogy of a "not-too-wide" corridor to describe the policy maker's conundrum. Policies that were too stimulating would only lead to more inflation and a future recession, but measures that didn't do enough would "leave the economic system far below what it might potentially be."[15] Moreover, Dunlop feared that continued high unemployment would strain the social fabric and the assorted institutions, including collective bargaining, that knitted it together.

Ford had created an Economic Policy Board to confront the dual problems of inflation and unemployment, and to serve as a central hub for the administration's economic policy. Unlike Nixon, who had relied almost entirely on his secretary of the treasury, George Shultz, for economic advice, President Ford was interested in an array of viewpoints and actively encouraged debate.[16] Whereas in the Nixon administration, Shultz and other close aides had tightly controlled the flow of economic data that reached the Oval Office, Ford's innovation was to involve multiple cabinet level people along with members of his economic team in decision making. As Bill Seidman, who served as an economic advisor to Ford, explained in a 1985 interview, the board represented an attempt to elevate the government's response to economic problems to the level of contingency planning associated with military problems. "Our job was to try and spot economic problems before they occurred and prepare a rational response to each problem," recalled Seidman.[17]

Dunlop was obviously part of the Economic Policy Board; Seidman maintains that he made his acceptance of Ford's offer of the secretary of labor position conditional upon that. And yet his approach to economic problem solving was in many ways counter to that embodied by the board. Just as Dunlop tried to impress upon his journalist "students" that there wasn't a silver-bullet fix for inflation and unemployment, he sought to convince fellow board members that there wasn't an "economy" per se, but a complex constellation of sectors, including food, housing and manufacturing. These sectors were in turn impacted by developments and forces that were often unpredictable, such as the international political developments that had sent oil prices soaring, or the crushing debt levels that had sent New York City to the brink of bankruptcy. There was no silver bullet, Dunlop maintained, because the economist's fiscal and monetary tools simply weren't adequate anymore. The solution was to "restore policy-making to the area of an art, to a series of negotiations, to consensus-building," he wrote.[18]

Then there was the problem of politics. The Economic Policy Board's *raison d'etre* was to intervene in economic problems before they escalated, potentially derailing the Ford Administration, which was keenly focused on the '76 primaries and the general election. Not only was Dunlop resistant to the idea of short-term fixes, he felt strongly that economic policy shouldn't be "the plaything of politicians." But he was keenly aware that Ford's political prospects hinged on his ability to bring down the rate of unemployment. Dunlop calculated that some 3.2 million new jobs were needed just to return unemployment to the level of the previous year, and then an additional 2 million jobs per year until 1980 to accommodate new entrants into the workforce. Ford's hands were effectively tied, wrote Dunlop. "If he gradually stimulated, he'd be criticized by the Democrats for not doing enough about unemployment. But if he super-stimulated he risked inflation and being accused of playing politics."[19]

Meanwhile, there were plenty of political divisions, even among the president's economic advisors. The conservative voices on the board's executive committee, including William Simon, whom Ford had designated his chief economic spokesperson, were "violently opposed" to stimulative policies. "We have been heading in a dangerous direction—the danger of killing the system that has given us the highest standard of living in the world," Simon told the *New York Times*.[20] Alan Greenspan, the chairman of the Council of Economic Advisors, was primarily focused on rolling back what he termed the "federal spending juggernaut."[21] Their refusal to consider fiscal stimulus even as the recession deepened led Dunlop to wonder whether they cared about unemployment at all.

The Labor-Management Committee, which Dunlop chaired, also played a key role in advising the president. Ford had established the committee by executive order soon after assuming office, designating 16 representatives, half from labor, half from management, to work together to identify policies that would contribute to the country's long-term economic benefit. With its commitment to tripartism, the committee embodied Dunlopian thinking; establishing joint problem-solving bodies in specific sectors and industries was also part of its mission. Ford would often drop by the group's meetings, reported Dunlop, so as to gain an inside perspective on the economy. "It seems the President enjoys hearing from members of the Committee—practical people—about the state of each of the sectors with which they are associated and are familiar."[22]

Dunlop derived deep satisfaction from his work overseeing the Labor-Management Committee, and it's not hard to see why. A typical session started with each group member reporting on the state of the economy—orders, inventory and price, employment figures—as seen from the vantage point of a particular sector or industry. The union chiefs provided additional information on unemployment and worker recalls. "That portion of the meeting is always particularly interesting because it provides absolutely current information from those people who are directly involved," observed Dunlop.[23] The remainder of the time was devoted to whatever group members felt was important. Only rarely was an agenda prepared in advance; such a thing wouldn't be worth much, Dunlop noted, "in a committee of such individualists who choose to run their discussion in their own ways."[24]

While the committee was intended to provide President Ford with advice, it differed from a typical advisory body in key respects. Its emphasis on seeking out pragmatic solutions to the biggest economic problems of the day assumed a willingness on the part of participants to change their own positions. These "constructive developments," as Dunlop often referred to them, depended on privacy, another distinguishing element of the body. The Labor-Management Committee was the only such White House convening that made a point of keeping its dealings out of the press. "No account of the discussion, no account of the conclusions or recommendation of the Committee leak into the press, and that's because the people keep their mouths shut," Dunlop noted.[25] As he understood from his years of labor negotiations and dispute resolution, the assorted parties couldn't change their positions unless they had confidence of an agreement being reached at some stage. The context was different but the principle here was exactly the same. The kind of accommodation necessary to address challenges in wage and price controls, economic and tax policy, simply wasn't possible "under the full blast of publicity and in public," Dunlop argued.[26]

The Labor-Management Committee would prove to be highly influential during Dunlop's brief tenure at the Department of Labor. The wisdom of its "practical people" was at least partially responsible for allowing Ford to break from the strict anti-inflationary position endorsed by his conservative advisors. Early in 1975, Ford announced his backing of fiscal stimulus, what would ultimately take the form of tax cuts targeted at lower and middle-income Americans and an extension of unemployment compensation to more workers, paired with a reduction in long-term federal spending. While Dunlop pronounced himself pleased with Ford's new direction, he noted with some frustration in his diary that just a single network had carried the president's speech announcing the change. He suspected that it had to do with the Equal Time rule, a classic example of regulatory overreach, or as he put it, "the ridiculous position that we've worked ourselves into."[27]

THE FIXER

Many of the problems that Dunlop confronted at the Department of Labor were what he thought of as "short-run" questions—the government equivalent of fires that had to be put out. Dunlop's goal was to solve both the challenge at hand and to construct the sort of mechanism necessary to ensure longer-term solutions. The Russian grain issue, for example, involved a relatively technical dispute over Russian imports of American wheat, necessitated by a dramatic plunge in the Russian grain crop. But Cold War politics made the issue seem intractably complicated. The president had previously come out against export controls, and many of his supporters were opposed to any kind of government intervention in the market. On the other side of the debate was AFL-CIO chief George Meany, whose rhetoric against the companies dealing directly with the Russians had grown increasingly sharp since the run-up in food prices in 1972. If the US sold to the Russians anywhere near the amount of grain they were requesting, even a small price increase in US markets would quickly become fodder for Ford's political opponents.

By late summer of 1975, the conflict threatened to boil over with American longshoremen refusing to load grain onto ships headed to Russia. Now in addition to the question of how much grain the US might sell to the Soviets, there was a labor dispute that threatened to disrupt an entire industry. Dunlop supported a long-term solution to the "grain issue"; he saw in the Russian's desperation an opportunity to gain leverage in future political dealings including arms-reduction talks. But he was also eager to develop a fix to prevent against just this kind of explosive conflict involving government maritime policy and the labor unions affected by it. Had there been some type of forum to which the unions could have brought their complaints, the job action might have been avoided, Dunlop observed. His influence was apparent in the final agreement, which included a five-year grain sales deal with the Russians and a tripartite committee involving labor, management and government representatives aimed at resolving problems in government maritime policy and facilitating constructive communications. To the short-run problem of Cold War-era grain sales, he had made what he hoped would be a longer-term contribution.

Dunlop took a similar approach to the long-running debate over US withdrawal from the International Labor Organization, the UN agency dealing with labor problems and international labor standards. In 1970, the US had cut its financial contribution to the ILO in half to protest the appointment of an Assistant-Director General who was from the Soviet Union. By the time Dunlop was tasked with cutting ties with the organization, the matter had become, as he saw it, mired in the messy business of money and politics. While withdrawal was a certainty, given that it was a top priority of the AFL-CIO's Meany, Dunlop once again sought to make the process as strategic as possible. Much of the controversy regarding the body, for example, had to do with the question of how "tripartite" it really was when the communist countries that held increasing sway lacked independent unions. Even as he performed the delicate dance of extracting the US from the organization, Dunlop noted in his diary that he was searching for a longer-term solution that would return the ILO to its "original first principles...eliminat[ing] a number of its more political elements and double standards, which have become more prominent in recent years."[28]

Even a labor dispute within the Department of Labor itself presented an occasion to transform a short-run issue into a constructive solution for the future. In the final weeks of Dunlop's time in Washington, labor tensions erupted in the building's restaurant, which was run by Stouffer's, using non-union workers. This was, Dunlop recognized, a source of trouble that had become a "festering problem." Labor leaders couldn't be invited to the Department of Labor for lunch, for example. And were a picket line to appear, the department would be virtually off limits to elected officials who were loathe to be seen crossing one. After workers at the restaurant announced their intention to organize a union and Stouffer's fired several of them, the potential picket lines became real. As Dunlop saw it, the conflict had resulted not just as a result of tensions between the union and Stouffer's, but between the union and the General Services Agency (GSA), which had assigned the contract in the first place. Even as he and his aides focused on defusing the immediate labor strife, Dunlop was working to improve communications and relations between the union and the GSA.

To each of these problems, Dunlop brought a similar perspective. Conflict, as he saw it, was typically the result of a breakdown in communication. Forums that encouraged and facilitated the exchange of information between parties—labor and management, with government providing mediation services—helped to prevent labor strife. And if "free and frank" conversation was the solution, the reliance on regulation represented the opposite in Dunlop's mind. In place of parties seeking to persuade one another in order to arrive at a mutually agreeable compromise, government technocrats were imposing rules. He had kicked off his "tour of duty" with a warning about regulatory overreach and his time in office only deepened his concern regarding what he saw as a hostility at the government level towards developing consensus and common views. "There is in this country a grossly exaggerated sense of what can be done by law, what can be done by ordering people around, what can be done by pieces of paper," Dunlop observed in September of 1975.[29]

This disconnect was further exacerbated by the vast distance between the bureaucrats whose job it was to regulate and the individuals who were most affected by the regulations. Just as President Ford had benefited immensely from the input of "practical people" from labor and industry, government agencies needed to involve the parties and people who would have to live under their handiwork. People who were entirely disassociated from the process would "seek continually to attack, to violate, to get around regulations that are promulgated," wrote Dunlop. "There is no administrator smart enough to write any set of regulations that others cannot find their ways around, through, over and under."[30] The inevitable consequence of what he called "pursuing government by regulation" was litigation—a loathsome by-product that served no one, save for the lawyers themselves. Why, he wondered, was there so much resistance to involving:

> more participation, more concentral understanding, more willingness to work problems out as distinct from the litigious character of issuing proposed regulations and contentiousness ending in endless lawsuits with nothing settled for many, many years followed by endless interpretations and political fights on the Hill, again, on amendments and 'round and 'round the mulberry bush.[31]

TAKING STOCK

Dunlop's brief tenure as secretary of labor is mostly remembered for how it ended: with his dramatic decision to resign after Ford's veto of so-called situs picketing legislation, the subject of the next chapter. But as his own chronicle of the period indicates, Dunlop's priorities extended far beyond efforts to get legislation favored by the building trades unions enacted into law. In the last pages of his diary, which he concluded soon after submitting his resignation to President Ford, Dunlop took stock of his time in office. He gave the issues that dominated his to-do list for nine months a glancing treatment, focusing instead upon his style of work—the particular sensibility that he brought to the job. He had tried to make longer term contributions to short-run problems, he noted, referencing the Russian grain crisis, regulatory reform, even the restaurant wars at the Department of Labor.

Two months after his swearing in Dunlop was asked by a White House fellow how much control of his department he had. Dunlop took the opportunity to explain to the gentleman that the very question represented a misunderstanding. There were the appointments he'd been making, the most obvious measure of Dunlop's influence, but "control" of the Department was also dependent upon his relationships with groups outside of it: labor unions, civil rights organizations, etc. Control, Dunlop maintained, should be understood as something that emerged as a result of trust, confidence, loyalty, and ideally, intellectual persuasion, rather than "as something which one captures or which one exerts by right or by authority."[32]

Of course, exercising the kind of intellectual and moral leadership that inspired respect and deference was no small task, Dunlop conceded in the final pages of his diary. One had only to look as far as President Ford's last-minute decision to veto legislation expanding the rights of construction workers to picket job sites, despite having given every indication to the contrary to labor leaders. "It is the crisis that tests men's souls and qualities," wrote Dunlop, "and I do not like what I see in the response of this President to this crisis."[33]

NOTES

1. Victor Riesel, "Dunlop Labor's Choice for Job," syndicated column, March 28, 1975.
2. Ibid.
3. Bruce E. Kaufman, "Reflections on Six Decades in Industrial Relations: An Interview with John Dunlop." *Industrial and Labor Relations Review* 55, no. 2 (January 2002): 326.
4. Ibid, 335.
5. Ibid.
6. Riesel, "Dunlop Labor's Choice for Job."
7. Gerald R. Ford," Remarks at the Swearing In of John T. Dunlop as Secretary of Labor," March 18, 1975.
8. Ibid.
9. John T. Dunlop, personal diary, April 6, 1975–February 26, 1976, sec. 2, 4.
10. Diary, sec. 2, 3.
11. Ibid., sec. 1, p. 7.
12. Ibid., sec. 11, 1.
13. Ibid., sec. 2, 5.
14. Ibid., sec. 11, 35.
15. Ibid., sec. 8,10–11.
16. Philip Shabecoff, "Attacks Mount on Ford Economic Policy," *New York Times*, November, 24, 1974.
17. Interview with L. William Seidman. Conducted by William A. Syres, Deputy Director, House Republican Policy Committee, June 12, 1985, 1. http://3197d6d14b5f19f2f440-5e13d29c4c016cf96cbbfd197c579b45.r81.cf1.rackcdn.com/collection/papers/1980/1985_0612_SeidmanSyers.pdf
18. Diary, sec. 12, 8.
19. Ibid., sec. 8, 11.
20. Shabecoff, "Attacks Mount on Ford Economic Policy."

21. Ibid.
22. Diary, sec. 13, 22.
23. Ibid., sec. 10, 31.
24. Ibid.
25. Ibid., sec. 13, 24.
26. Ibid., sec. 8, 2.
27. Ibid., sec. 11, 20.
28. Ibid., sec. 10, 14.
29. Ibid., sec. 10, 26.
30. Ibid., sec. 9, 17.
31. Ibid., sec. 13, 24.
32. Ibid., sec. 5,10.
33. Ibid., sec 16, 95.

Chapter Four

Dead on Arrival

On December 11 of 1975, John Dunlop was summoned to the White House for a meeting on the fate of a bill on so-called common situs picketing. The measure, which would allow a strike against one subcontractor on a construction site to shut down the entire site, had passed the House earlier that fall and appeared likely to squeak through the Senate. But the president, who'd publicly stated his support for situs, had come under ferocious pressure from a newly aggressive business lobby and a right wing on the rise, complete with its own presidential candidate, Ronald Reagan. During the meeting with Ford and a young staff member named Dick Cheney, Dunlop repeated the case he'd been making for weeks: that the legislation was far less favorable to the unions than it had been, that it would be phased in gradually, and that 90 percent of the homebuilding industry would be exempted. President Ford appeared persuaded by these arguments, Dunlop noted in a diary entry. Then the conversation turned to politics. By the time the hour-long session wrapped up, Dunlop understood that, if the legislation made it to his desk, the Ford planned to veto it, leaving Dunlop with no choice but to resign.[1]

It seems hard to fathom now, more than four decades removed, that something called common situs picketing was once a topic of intense national debate, if not quite a household term. Legalizing "situs" had been a priority for the buildings trades unions for decades, since the Supreme Court had ruled that each contractor on a construction site was a separate entity, covered by a separate labor agreement. The so-called Denver decision prohibited unions from picketing general contractors who hired nonunion workers. Year after year, the building trade unions had argued that the ruling discriminated against construction workers. Industrial workers, they pointed out, were entitled to picket entire factories. But in 1975, pressure to do something about the prohibition against situs picketing was building, and this time the argument had new force behind it.

The construction boom, which had fueled the torrid pace of wage increases that Dunlop's Construction Industry Stabilization Commission had sought to keep a lid on in 1971, had fizzled by 1973. Building in everything from housing to commercial construction to highway projects and electric utility work dried up, with the result that unemployment among construction workers was soaring. By 1975, their unemployment rate stood at 22 percent, twice as high as the national average. The problem was even more severe in major cities, where as many as half of the workers who laid brick, built frames and carried out the heavy lifting of all kinds had no work. As Robert Georgine, head of the AFL-CIO's Building and Construction Trades Department, told delegates to the group's convention in 1975, "Our task is to . . . devise means of escape from the economic swamp in which we are expiring."[2] The solution, Georgine was convinced, lay in the long-awaited passage of the Equal Treatment of Craft and Industrial Workers Bill, aka common situs picketing.

While Dunlop had doubts as to the wisdom of launching another legislative campaign around the issue, he was largely in agreement with the unions that the Court's decision was fundamentally flawed. On many job sites, contractors worked together, supervised by a general contractor or project manager. "[T]here's a significant commonality of interest among them and what one craft does often has an impact on others," Dunlop observed. "Thus, when the Court tries to treat each contractor as independent it is not being very realistic—it is not recognizing that the crafts all work together as a whole."[3] Moreover, the "fictitious world of gates" that the National Labor Relations Board and the courts had imposed upon construction sites was an example of just the kind regulatory overreach that Dunlop saw as such a problem.[4]

Dunlop also recognized an opportunity to pursue much needed structural reforms within the construction industry. Thus, the legislation that would begin to take shape in the fall of 1975 was actually two bills: the "situs" relief sought by the building trades, and collective bargaining reform. Employers were understandably concerned that picketing would lead to more strikes, driving up costs as a result. Dunlop was largely sympathetic to this concern. Wage spikes in the construction industry had been a major contributor to the 1970's inflation scourge, and the autonomous structure of the unions themselves was largely to blame. When a particular local decided that it wanted a pay raise and was willing to suspend work in order to get it, the international union lacked the authority to stop it. "Dunlop knew that the solution was to centralize more power in the building trades unions," recalls Hank Perritt, who had rejoined Dunlop's staff at the Department of Labor after working with him at the Cost of Living Council. "The international presidents certainly weren't opposed to having more power."[5]

POSITIVE PROGNOSIS

As Dunlop recounts in his 2002 interview, the assumption that the construction legislation was a priority for him was a misconception; it had been Ford's idea.[6] In fact, as Dunlop makes clear in his personal journal, working with the legislature was far and away the least appealing part of his job as secretary of labor. "Legislative sausage making left little opportunity for philosophical consideration of the issues underlying the topics of the day," he wrote.[7] While there were certainly matters of great substance reflected in the situs legislation, for example, the process of government policy formulation seemed intent on avoiding them. "These issues of jurisdiction are those which seem to concern and excite government officials the most, I regret to say."[8] Despite his frustration with the legislative process, he approached the task at hand with the same big-picture perspective that characterized his other work at the department. As Dunlop saw it, situs legislation represented an opportunity to deal with endemic problems within the construction industry, including fragmentation among the contractors. If ever there was a sector that could benefit from tripartite style problem-solving, he was convinced, it was construction.

By September of 1975, Dunlop reported feeling positive about the prospects of the construction legislation. While AFL-CIO chief George Meany had initially balked at the collective bargaining reform elements of the bill, railing against what he saw as government legislating arrangements between local and national unions, his opposition had softened as passage of a key union priority seemed finally to be in reach. Even the contractors, who were overwhelmingly Republican, appeared to have met their match in President Ford. When the contractors demanded to know why Congress was considering providing support for situs at a time when construction worker wages were still rising despite high unemployment, Ford had a simple answer. Congress was responsive to the labor movement because labor had invested the funds to get members elected. "It is still too soon to prognosticate how all this will come out," wrote Dunlop, "but I guess one would have to say that things have gone a lot faster and by much wider margins than might have previously been thought possible with respect to both of these matters earlier in the year."[9]

By the time the legislation came up for a vote in the House, it had undergone extensive modifications. New provisions essentially eliminated strikes for any cause, while an array of other issues, including grievances and secondary boycotts had to be resolved through arbitration if an agreement couldn't be reached. Similar to the project labor agreements the federal government had adopted in its space and missile building sites in the 1960's, "[t]he effect would be to make the industry strike free," explained Dunlop.[10] The changes were enough to win over skittish legislators, while the unions, victory tantalizing close at last, had made significant concessions. "John would often say that some people sign an agreement smiling, some people sign an agreement holding their noses," recalls Dunlop's long-time colleague Quinn Mills.[11] The legislation that the press referred to as the "Picket Bill" fit both of those descriptions.

STORM CLOUDS GATHERING

Even as the legislation made its way through Congress, there were gathering signs of trouble on the horizon. Opposition from conservative organizations and corporate leaders, who believed that the bill was heavily tilted in favor of the unions, was intensifying. Situs was opposed across the construction industry, by the National Association of Manufacturers and the Chamber of Commerce. "The principle reason for labor's seeking this weapon of common situs is an organizing tool," said an official of the Associated General Contractors of America, which represented both union and nonunion contractors. "We think it goes pretty deep into the freedom of choice of both workers and management."[12]

The public was increasingly weighing in too. During the months-long debate over the Picket Bill, the White House received some 700,000 pieces of correspondence about the issue, many of them echoing pro-industry claims.[13] In November, Dunlop himself received one of these: a letter from conservative Arizona Senator Paul Fannin, "in a special type form and sent out to individuals as is the wont today of our political and lobbying processes." [14] The letter even called out Dunlop himself as the chief architect of "this ill-conceived legislation," maintaining that Ford had been poised to wield his veto pen till his secretary of labor had persuaded him otherwise. If Dunlop and his "labor friends" got their way, Fannin predicted ominously, building and construction costs would skyrocket, sending inflation skyward with tax rates sure to follow. "Every worker in those trades will be forced to pay union dues and fees or join the ranks of the unemployed. Millions of dollars more will pour into the union treasuries, money that will be spent to defeat any free enterprise candidate who dares to stand up against union bosses' demands," Fannin warned.[15]

The lobbying campaign was like nothing Dunlop had ever seen before: intense, emotional and lavishly funded by industry groups. Yet he continued to hold out hope that cooler heads would prevail, and that construction industry leaders would be called upon to stop exaggerating the consequences of the legislation. Dunlop also reached out to his contacts within various contractors' groups to talk "dispassionately" about what he was convinced were misconceptions regarding the likelihood that the legislation would lead to greater inflation. But his efforts came to naught, and by mid-November, he and his staff and colleagues watched in dismay as one newspaper editorial board after another echoed the claims being made by Senator Fannin and other opponents of the legislation.

The intense pressure was clearly taking a toll on President Ford, not to mention his poll numbers. Situs was suddenly an issue on the campaign trail as Reagan courted the same conservative and pro-business voters who saw the legislation as a sop to the unions. On December 11, Dunlop was summoned to meet with Ford, who described the dilemma he faced. While he had no problem with the merits of the bill, its "political aspects" were keeping him up at night; he simply hadn't anticipated the force of the opposition from the conservative flank of his own party. "Men whom he had known for many, many years who every time they see him have been simply riding him very, very hard on the question of situs picketing and that it was unthinkable that he would sign the legislation," Ford told Dunlop.[16] But then there was the pledge that Ford had made to the AFL-CIO's Robert Georgine, whom he considered a personal friend. "He had always lived by the motto that a man's word was his bond," recounts Dunlop.[17]

Ford was put in an impossible position, recalls Quinn Mills, who had taken over for Dunlop as the chair of the Construction Industry Stabilization Committee. Ford had made a commitment to the building trades unions, whose support he needed to be reelected, but the employers represented his natural constituency as a Republican. "The employers realized that their last line of defense was the president," says Mills. "They went to him and basically what they said is that if you sign this bill, we will not support you, and you will not be re-nominated."[18]

As Ford indicated in the December 11 meeting, he was all too aware of how the intense debate was playing out in key primary states. Situs would likely not be an issue in New Hampshire, he said, but would be a problem in Florida and North Carolina, where party chairmen and fundraisers for his campaign were sending ominous signals that they planned to bolt if Ford signed the bill into law. In Iowa, meanwhile, the farmers were unhappy about the Russian grain issue, grumbling that Ford was in the pocket of George Meany. What worried Ford most of all, recounted Dunlop, was that the GOP would nominate Ronald Reagan, while the Democrats picked another extreme candidate, leaving the American people in the unfortunate position of "choosing between two extremes." There were Democrats who Ford indicated wouldn't disturb him if they were to run, recounts Dunlop. "but the campaign to be run between two extremists was of major concern to him."[19]

DONE DEAL

If Ford had already made up his mind to veto the legislation, he didn't let on during that meeting. But he and Dunlop were already discussing the implications of a veto for Dunlop himself, namely the question of whether Ford's secretary of labor would have no choice but to resign. For Dunlop, there appears to have been little question. In their conversation, he flashed back to the previous year, when, with Don Rumsfeld present, Ford had asked him to take the job. The president's top priority had been establishing open and direct communication with labor. A veto of situs would make impossible the kind of constructive conversations that Dunlop had spent the previous months facilitating. "It would, in effect, put up a curtain between the Federation and other unions...and the Administration," said Dunlop.[20] And just as Dunlop's own job would be made impossible, any chance of Ford "breaching" labor ranks in support of his candidacy was gone as well. Nixon's efforts to win key labor support in his 1972 bid for re-election had collapsed after the administration's imposition of wage controls and suspension of the Davis-Bacon Act on federal projects. A veto of situs would have a similar effect, warned Dunlop, turning potential supporters into sworn enemies.

A few days later, the legislation squeaked through the Senate by a vote of 52–43, but it was quickly pronounced dead on arrival by the press. As the *New York Times* reported, among Ford's top economic and political advisers, only the secretary of labor remained publicly supportive of the bill.[21] Dunlop was certainly aware of his growing isolation. After yet another White House meeting, two days after the bill's passage, Dunlop described feeling that there was "very great hostility" on the part of the Ford's staff to the bill.[22] Nor did he have any luck with a last ditch effort to convince members of the Economic Policy Board that the veto would mean more turmoil in the construction industry as bitter unions clashed with the contractors group, grown "newly arrogant over its unexpected victory." Both the volume of strikes and the size of settlements were likely to be destabilizing, he warned the group, but to no discernable effect. "While the Board members all had very strong opinions, they didn't seem to know anything," observed Dunlop.[23]

FALLOUT

The evening of December 22 found Dunlop at the Black Horse Tavern, a regular meeting spot of his, joined by AFL-CIO lieutenant Tom Donahue. President Ford had made a public announcement regarding his decision to veto the situs legislation earlier that day. With the assistance of his communications aide, Dick Lukstat, Dunlop had crafted a response for the inevitable press inquiries. He was disappointed in the president's veto; he felt the two bills had represented a constructive step, and he had followed the president's instructions throughout. As for his own plans, Dunlop would be taking two to three weeks to consult with labor and management representatives before making any kind of official announcement about his future. Now, as Dunlop and Donahue concluded their discussion of the day's disappointing events, Lukstat and John Read joined them, bringing with them the text of the president's full veto statement.

Ford had gone out of his way to praise his secretary of labor and his abilities, before laying out his primary rationale for opposing the legislation. The construction bills, Ford stated, were likely to increase disputes within the construction industry. "Nothing could be further from the truth," wrote Dunlop.[24]

The president's decision had come down to politics—to a handful of primary states—and yet from Dunlop's vantage point, the political fallout from the veto was likely to be profound. Ford's hope that he could win over conservative building trades voters was officially dead. The unions would now "vigorously, and with enthusiasm, attack him at every turn." And the prospects for what he termed "constructive developments" in labor-management relations more generally, had just dimmed considerably too. From the Labor-Management Committee to the Construction Committee to the ongoing conversations about the International Labor Organization, Dunlop had deployed a similar approach: convince the parties to restrain whatever animus they felt in the spirit of trying to work the various problems out. Instead of the improved communication between government, management and unions that he had come on board to facilitate, Dunlop was convinced that the year ahead was likely to see a sharp uptick in labor strife. "All in all, not a pretty picture, but no one can ever say that the president has not been fully, completely warned about it in some detail."[25]

Despite Dunlop's statement to the press that he was mulling over his future, he saw no alternative but to step down. When he met with Ford's economic advisor, Bill Seidman, Dunlop was forthright about what the president's veto meant for him personally. He'd been asked by the president to carry out a particular set of assignments, and the president himself had now created conditions that made carrying out those assignments with any degree of success impossible.[26] Beyond that, however, as Dunlop made clear to Seidman in terms that he conceded were "pretty rough," he no longer trusted Ford. "I told him categorically that the president had double-crossed everyone involved; that that sort of behavior was not one that inspired confidence."[27]

Dunlop returned home to Belmont for Christmas, but his hopes for a quiet gathering with his family were soon dashed. President Ford had made a further statement about his decision to veto situs while on a holiday visit to Vail, Colorado, reiterating his high regard for his secretary of labor and expressing his hopes that Dunlop would stay on. As a result, the phone at the Belmont house was ringing constantly. The calls came from management representatives alarmed at the prospect that he might quit, from his labor friends who believed that he had no choice but to leave, and from journalists who wanted to know what his plans were. To the latter group, Dunlop stuck to the messaging that he and Lukstat had developed together. Not even Tom Brokaw could get him to reveal more than that, Dunlop noted. On Christmas day he put an end to the calls.[28]

But even as he relaxed with his family, Dunlop was mulling over the future. Giving up government service entirely would mean that there would be virtually no one left at the highest levels who believed in collective bargaining, or even understood why it was necessary. "Unions are viewed, on the whole, as unnecessary appendages and people would wish that they go away," he reflected.[29] The AFL-CIO's Lane Kirkland shared his concern and encouraged Dunlop to focus on how best to be of service to labor and management in the future, rather than focusing on the short-term concerns of the moment. Other labor leaders had encouraged him to stay in office, "a known person is much better . . . than someone new," as the UAW's Leonard Woodcock put it—a line of reasoning that Dunlop had rejected as unimpressive.[30] Tellingly, Dunlop considered the question of what to do next in classic Dunlopian style, consulting widely with labor and management leaders regarding what, if any, prospects there were for constructive developments in the labor-management field. Those conversations led him to conclude that such prospects were bleak. "[A]ttitudes have been significantly affected and . . . the requisite communications, confidence and trust, is no longer possible, at least with me in the post of Secretary of Labor."[31]

In the solitude of his home office, he drafted his letter of resignation until it had the tone he was after: "moderate," and focused "squarely on the basis of the incapacity to do the assignment which the president asked me to do."[32] The document proved easy enough to write; it was the question of how to handle his deep disappointment in Ford himself that was so confounding for Dunlop. As he had indicated in his conversation with Bill Seidman, and in his exchanges with Robert Georgine and George Meany, he believed that Ford had gone back on his word. But even more than the "double cross" was what the incident revealed about Ford's own character. Dunlop believed Ford's statement that the decision over whether to veto situs was the toughest he'd ever faced. Ford faced a tension between having given his word on the one hand and the internal politics of his party and the threat of Ronald Reagan on the other. And he'd chosen politics. "The episode is extremely revealing as to the decision-making process and internal moral quality of the President," Dunlop concluded.[33]

Dunlop found some solace and perspective in history. He spent a few days reading the spring '75 issue of *Daedalus*, the Journal of the American

Arts and Sciences Society. The issue was entitled "Wisdom, Revelation and Doubt: Perspectives on the First Millennium BC," and explored why the great sets of moral and ethical views of society had emerged at the same time. He also talked to his long-time colleagues at Harvard: Derek Bok, Franklin Ford, who'd been his predecessor as Dean of the Faculty of Arts and Sciences, and Larry Fouraker, the Dean of the Harvard Business School. On Christmas night, Bok stopped by the Dunlop home, bearing a cake that he'd baked with his daughter. "I must confess that it was a marvelous cake," Dunlop reported. He pronounced himself delighted that Bok and his other Harvard colleagues, with whom he'd been through so much "university travail," would think of his problems on this occasion.[34]

GOING PUBLIC

Dunlop's official submission of his resignation was an anticlimactic affair compared to the events that preceded it. On the afternoon of January 13, 1976, he was summoned to a meeting at the White House with President Ford. Dunlop had already indicated to Dick Cheney that he planned to take a "high road" approach to the occasion, and that's exactly what he did. The letter he'd penned was short and to the point; he presented it to Ford along with a brief explanation of his decision. The question before him was 'what could be done constructively in the period ahead?' The answer was "not much." Ford, by contrast, had come armed with a long list of reasons why Dunlop should stay. Chief among them: that Dunlop's "practical," "persuasive" and "common sense" perspective was essential to the work of the Economic Policy Board.[35]

They also revisited, one last time, the politics of the president's decision. Ford insisted that he *had* taken labor's hostile reaction into account but was convinced it would pass before the election, adding that he'd always believed labor people to be "patriotic Americans" who would "set aside political differences in order to get along with the main business of the country."[36] Privately, Dunlop regarded this as one of the strangest statements he'd ever heard Ford make, but he responded simply that for the unions to reverse a position they'd taken publicly seemed highly unlikely. He made one final attempt to impress upon Ford the consequences of "having brought the curtain down" between labor and his administration, reminding the president of the chill between George Meany and the previous labor secretary that Ford had brought in Dunlop to thaw. And that was it. The final meeting between the president and his secretary of labor was cordial and free of rancor. As Dunlop described it: "I tried in every way possible to show my respect and my desire to be accommodating within the limits and the realities of a resignation."[37]

The following day, Dunlop made the news public, reading the statement he'd crafted so carefully, then taking questions from reporters. The smoothness of the event reflected weeks of work on the part of his tight-knit staff. Exceptionally close to his "team of tigers," Dunlop had relied upon them even more since the president had announced his decision to veto situs. Hank Perritt, John Read, Dick Lukstat and Bob Aders had worked tirelessly to assist Dunlop in exiting the position on his own terms and completing the substantive work of regulatory reform that he'd embarked upon 10 months before. To prepare for the press conference, Lukstat and the others had given Dunlop questions to consider, and more importantly, to help him get into the right frame of mind around the event. Their preparation paid off; several reporters commented upon the fact that Dunlop seemed very relaxed. Meanwhile the question that had most concerned him—would he be supporting President Ford politically in the year ahead?—hadn't come up.[38]

In his statement, Dunlop referenced his discussions with a wide variety of labor and management leaders, and his "sober conclusion" that the required communications, confidence and trust needed for him to be an effective secretary of labor was gone. Left unmentioned was another key element: his loss of regard for his boss. In the period following Ford's decision to veto situs, Dunlop's assessment of the man only seems to have grown darker. Dunlop was convinced that Ford had made the wrong decision, and by using a phony rationale to justify it had revealed in the process that his word didn't mean much. "It is the crisis that tests men's souls and qualities, and I do not like what I see in the response of this President to this crisis. How would he react in other crises? How does he face up to issues of tough policy?" wondered Dunlop.[39] In an effort to fend off the right wing of his party, Ford had done nothing but demonstrate his subservience to it, something that Dunlop found, in his words, "enormously disturbing."[40]

END OF THE TOUR

In preparing for his imminent departure, Dunlop looked to a most unlikely role model: Nathan Pusey, who'd been forced to retire as president of Harvard University as a result of the political turmoil that had subsumed the campus in 1969. Pusey, Dunlop noted, had used the final days of his tenure to make the sorts of hard decisions that Harvard's leaders had tended to avoid. In a private meeting with colleagues, recalls Dunlop, Pusey encouraged them to propose matters that needed to be done; they could then blame such "nasty decisions" on him.[41] Dunlop approached his final two weeks in office with this point of view in mind, taking what he hoped would be definitive action on some of the thorniest issues on his plate: the exit of the US from the International Labor Organization, affirmative action in higher education, and a simmering controversy within the steel industry over coke oven standards. As Dunlop indicated to his closest associates—Read, Perritt, Lukstat and Aders among them—he was willing to make hard decisions that might be difficult for his successor, Bill Usery, to make.

Of course, two weeks wasn't much time, which meant that Dunlop's "tiered style" meetings—a cocktail round, a dinner round, a final 'holding-forth' round—required additional tiers to accommodate all of the necessary conversations. The final pages of his diary are peppered with the names of Washington watering holes and eateries where he conducted business, engaged in negotiations and tended to the relationships that were at the very core of his work. In between the meetings with labor and government officials and management representatives were a few that merited special attention. One such occasion: dinner with *New York Times* editor Jimmy Reston, at whose suggestion Dunlop had embarked on his written record of his time in office. They enjoyed a long chat about the Washington world in a general and philosophical way, reported Dunlop. As for the journal itself, Dunlop feared that he had "not adequately taken the time to talk about the foibles of personality and characteristics of people as individuals to the extent that [Reston] would like."[42]

One of the last items on Dunlop's calendar before he returned to Massachusetts was a final session of the weekly seminar for reporters he'd begun while at the Cost of Living Council and had resumed as secretary of labor. At these regular gatherings, offered to 20–25 representatives of major newspapers and media outlets, and developed in response to requests from the reporters themselves, Dunlop would spend 15 or 20 minutes addressing key economics and policy questions for the press. During the rest of the hour, the "students" could question their "professor." The goal, said Dunlop, was "to develop an informed level of information, background, critical capacity and analytical discussion" among the press. If journalists had a greater understanding of issues, he insisted, they would be less likely to misconstrue specific developments in the quest for headlines.[43]

The last session of the class was a graduation of sorts. After lunch at the National Press Club, Dunlop handed out certificates of completion for what he called a "Correspondent's Course," signed by him, using the title "Group Discussion Leader." The diplomas certified that the reporters had completed the course, more or less to his satisfaction.[44] Walt Mossberg, then the senior labor reporter for the Wall Street Journal, was on hand that day, as he had been for nearly every session of what he describes as this "strange class."[45] For Mossberg, who'd begun his reporting career covering the autoworkers in Detroit, Dunlop represented a refreshing, even surprising, change from the Washington-based labor organizations that he'd grown used to covering. There was the AFL, which to Mossberg resembled a medieval guild, and the Teamsters with their penchant for criminality. Then there was Dunlop.

"Here was this guy who I thought of as kind of an Ivory tower Brahmin who was able to talk to union people and cared about the success of the labor movement, but also about the health of the economy," recalls Mossberg.[46] "He had the respect of leaders in the building trades who didn't typically want anything to do with academics." While Mossberg has long since moved on from the labor beat, he says that he still recalls his "professor" with great fondness and admiration. "When people mention his name, I always smile inwardly and think kindly of the guy. I've seen a lot of public servants. Dunlop was among the best."[47]

The air at the press "graduation" was celebratory, as it was a few days later when Dunlop and 75 staff members and their spouses gathered at Washington DC's Tallow House for a reception and "period of humor." It was the same locale where he and his family had enjoyed a dinner to mark the occasion of his swearing in. Dunlop's staff presented him with a parting gift: the chair he'd used while in office. The following day, he returned to Belmont. He devoted the final entry of his diary to describing the trip: how in last of his weekly commutes between his two home bases, he'd gradually been returning the items from his DC apartment back to his Belmont home. On this trip he had somehow managed to bring on board the aircraft not just the sheets and blankets from his DC bed, but his bedspread. He remarked with great satisfaction that a colleague of his on the flight, Graham Allison, had had to wait to retrieve belongings for a mere one week stay, whereas Dunlop himself was moving "house and town" without checking any luggage at all.[48]

For all of the drama and political intrigue that precipitated Dunlop's decision to step down as secretary of labor, he reported feeling no regrets as he left Washington behind. "Basically I have no difficulty in looking in the mirror in the morning as I shave and have a sense of respect and no remorse over what has happened."[49] Well, there were a few disappointments. Among them: that in his final weeks, he had not been able to reach a resolution on OSHA's coke oven standard. The complex negotiations he'd been facilitating between the Steelworkers Union and the ten companies which did the principal bargaining in the steel industry had come to naught. The culprit was internal union politics, Dunlop noted, still hopeful that there would be some way to settle the matter in the future even if he was no longer in office.

NOTES

1. John T. Dunlop, personal diary, April 6, 1975–February 26, 1976, sec. 10–13, p. 17–18.

2. Grace Palladino, *Skilled Hands, Strong Spirits: A Century of Building Trades History*, (Ithaca, NY: Cornell University Press, 2005), 179–180.
3. Bruce Kaufman, "Reflections on Six Decades in Industrial Relations: An Interview with John Dunlop." *Industrial and Labor Relations Review*, 55, no. 2 (January 2002): 324–348.
4. Diary, sec. 12, 33.
5. Hank Perritt, interviewed by the author, January 18, 2016.
6. Kaufman, 342.
7. Diary, sec. 6, 21–22.
8. Ibid., sec. 10, 9.
9. Ibid., sec. 10, 28.
10. Marc Linder, *Wars of Attrition: Vietnam, the Business Roundtable and the Decline of Construction Unions*, (Iowa City, Iowa: Fanpihua Press, 2000), 334.
11. Quinn Mills, interviewed by the author, June 21, 2016.
12. Lee Dembart, "Issue and Debate," *New York Times*, November 6, 1975.
13. Cited in Mike Davis, *Prisoners of the American Dream: Politics and Economy in the History of the US Working Class*, (New York: Verso, 1986), p. 135.
14. Diary, sec. 14, 1.
15. Ibid., sec 14, 1–2.
16. Ibid., sec.16, 21.
17. Ibid., sec. 16,19.
18. Mills interview.
19. Diary, sec. 16, 23–24.
20. Ibid., sec. 13, 27.
21. David Rosenbaum, "Energy and Construction-Picket Bills are Approved," *New York Times*, December 16, 1975.
22. Diary, sec. 16, 64.
23. Ibid., sec. 13, 38–39.
24. Ibid., sec 16, 88.
25. Ibid.
26. As Dunlop notes, Seidman encouraged Dunlop to stay on if for no other reason than to exercise continued influence on the Economic Policy Board, where his "independent, strong" positions were needed to counter the conservatives on the Board, including Alan Greenspan. Diary, sec. 16, 90.
27. Diary, sec.16, 89.
28. Ibid., sec.16, 92.
29. Ibid., sec.17, 15.
30. Ibid., sec.17, 28.
31. Ibid., sec. 17, 72.
32. Ibid., sec. 16, 93–94.
33. Ibid., sec. 16, 94–95.
34. Ibid., sec. 16, 97.
35. Ibid., sec. 17, 64.
36. Ibid., sec. 17, 64–65.
37. Ibid., sec. 17, 64–69.
38. Ibid., sec. 17, 71–74.
39. Ibid., sec. 16, 95.
40. Ibid.
41. Ibid., sec. 17, 83.
42. Ibid., sec. 16, 101–103.
43. Ibid., sec. 2, 7.
44. Ibid., sec. 18, 14.
45. Walt Mossberg, interviewed by the author, October 31, 2016.
46. Ibid.
47. Ibid.
48. Diary, sec.18, p. 22.
49. Diary, sec.18, p. 1.

Chapter Five

At the Table

When Dunlop gave up his position as secretary of labor in January of 1976, he headed back to Harvard. But as he told a key group of fundraisers for the university shortly before his departure from Washington, he planned to settle in a new home at Harvard: the business school. As Dunlop explained to the money men, the move reflected his concerned with the role of business and management in society. "Not at the philosophical level of Schumpeter, who argued that capitalism was being killed by its own successes," said Dunlop.[1] His particular interest, by contrast, lay with the policies of business toward political processes in general. How did business decide whether to get into or stay out of politics? How would companies react to the growing tendency towards increased and increasingly detailed government regulation? Where did they look for alliances? What he wanted to understand, Dunlop said, was "what private business stood for in this country."[2]

Dunlop wasn't content to confine his inquiry to academic study. The new office on the campus of Harvard Business School would be his official base, but Dunlop was already thinking about how to return to Washington in order to facilitate "constructive conversations" between private business and labor groups. Even as he was winding down his "tour of duty" as secretary of labor, Dunlop began laying the groundwork to reconstitute the Labor-Management Committee. Ford's veto of the situs picketing legislation had effectively killed the group, but Dunlop hadn't given up on either the forum or the rationale behind it. Perhaps, he mused in a meeting with Bechtel executive Bret Hartford, it might be possible to arrange a meeting of the labor and business leaders from the Ford committee outside of government. The goal of this "quiet" convening would be "to begin to talk about long-run issues, and . . . create an atmosphere in which some constructive developments could take place."[3]

In the conclusion of the personal diary that he kept during his year as secretary of labor, Dunlop ranked the Labor-Management Committee up near the top of the list of what he termed areas of special interest for him. It's easy to see why. The gatherings provided an unparalleled glimpse into the workings, and more importantly, the shortcomings of the economy at a time of high inflation and persistent unemployment. Access to business leaders who knew exactly what was happening in their individual sectors provided Dunlop with key insights into the workings of the economy at a time when the process of gathering economic data remained highly cumbersome. Each week, the group members would report on orders, inventory and prices in their particular sectors, as well as unemployment and the recall of previously laid-off workers. Wrote Dunlop: "That portion of the meeting is always particularly interesting because it provides absolutely current information from those people who are directly involved." [4]

But the committee also represented the actualization of Dunlop's approach to economic problem solving and the philosophy he'd articulated at his swearing-in ceremony as secretary of labor. Here were business, labor, and government working together to respond to the nation's immediate problems—and its longer-term challenges." Here too was the mutual problem solving and informal mediation, facilitated by the government—exactly the role that Dunlop believed it should be playing. If law and regulation had replaced the old art of consensus, the Labor-Management Committee was a return to persuasion and accommodation. The group also embodied Dunlop's view of the economy, not as a monolith, but composed of sectors, geographic regions, and key industries, here represented by the individuals who understood them best.

The first iteration of the group had been set up by Dunlop and then Secretary of the Treasury George Shultz in 1973 while Dunlop was heading up the Cost of Living Council. Called the Labor-Management Advisory Committee, the group reflected Dunlop and Shultz's shared belief that economic policy required a "significant direct contribution" from labor and business communities.[5] The committee was also intended to function as a forum for an ongoing, and most importantly, frank conversation about the state of the economy during a time of tumult and conflict. And while the group would cease to function after the end of the stabilization program in 1974, its hiatus was brief. When President Ford asked Dunlop to recommend some members of a new body, what became the Labor-Management Committee looked very similar to the one Dunlop and Shultz had set up.

The group that Dunlop reconstituted in the early days of the Carter Administration included sixteen representatives of major unions and companies. Labor was represented by the AFL-CIO and by individual unions including the United Autoworkers and the Steelworkers. General Electric and US Steel, both of which had huge unionized workforces, were at the table, but so were corporate chiefs from companies like DuPont, CitiCorp and Sears Roebuck, which had no unions to speak of. But while this body resembled the one first convened by Richard Nixon and continued under President Ford, it differed in a key respect. Unlike the previous iterations, the Carter-era Labor-Management Group had no official advisory role but was considered "semi-official."

The difference in designation was key, Dunlop noted. For one, its business could be carried out in private, away from what he described as "the full blast of publicity and the public."[6] And whereas public negotiations meant "speechmaking," or worse, ideology, in Dunlop's opinion, the conversations that took place behind closed doors were aimed at changing the positions of the labor and management representatives. "[I]mplicit in any advice given is a willingness to openly support the position taken and to work legislatively or administratively or in other ways to achieve the results agreed upon."[7] Dunlop's description of the work of the group he'd presided over as secretary of labor indicates the promise he saw in this model of problem solving. Labor and management had to come together on the big issues of the day: taxation, economic policy, inflation. Here was a way of seeking out "pragmatic resolution and pragmatic solutions to very serious problems."[8]

The focus of the group went beyond just economic policy. Indeed, Dunlop's description of the interests under consideration included virtually every key national issue of the day. Among them were unemployment, jobs and capital formation, housing, the regulatory process, energy, New York City's financial problems, health care, Social Security, international trade, illegal aliens, agricultural policy, welfare, the balance of clean air and water, and the public understanding of collective bargaining.[9] For President Carter, however, it was the input on his new Labor-Management Group's input on one topic that seemed to matter most of all: inflation.

In July of 1977, Carter convened a major meeting of "inflation fighters": top economic officials from his own administration, along with Dunlop and other representatives of the Labor-Management Group. Reports from the closed-door affair at Washington's Hay-Adams Hotel revealed just how wary Carter's administration was of the inflation problem—and the extent to which Dunlop's belief in the potential of collaborative problem solving was now reflected in the highest reaches of officialdom. But the exercise represented more than a mere nod to collaboration. Built into the process was Dunlop's understanding of power dynamics. Labor unions and businesses had both been brought to the table by self-interest, the former fearing being blamed for high inflation driven by wage increases, the latter worried about inflationary price increases. The result was the creation of an instrument that might finally be to do something about inflation. Carter hoped, as *New York Times* writer Leonard Silk wrote, "that by a really deep exploration of the inflation problem in all its ramifications, working in close collaboration with business, better and more lasting answers can be evolved than any other Western nation has yet discovered."[10]

BITTER BATTLES

If Carter was banking on collaboration between labor unions and business to solve the country's economic woes, labor unions viewed the Labor-Management Group as important for a very different reason. They saw the group's corporate members as a key source of support for a package of labor bills that the AFL-CIO sought to push through Congress. In addition to revisiting "situs" legislation, labor groups also sought labor law reform, including an expansion of the National Labor Relations Board that the AFL-CIO hoped would counter growing efforts on the part of employers to thwart unionization. Meany and other labor leaders believed that the spirit of collaboration in Dunlop's new labor/management convening was representative of a larger shared commitment to economic prosperity, one that would ultimately show up in the form of the reform legislation's passage. Murray Finley of the Amalgamated Clothing and Textile Workers Union explained labor's view of the compact this way: "Labor would support free enterprise, and business would support a strong, democratic labor movement."[11]

But the recent demise of situs picketing legislation at the hands of a newly organized, newly aggressive business lobby points to the problem with this view. As the full-press campaign against situs had shown, business groups had come to see unions less as partners than as an expensive, outmoded adversary. In his book *Prisoners of the American Dream*, Mike Davis describes the irony that many of the same business leaders in Dunlop's new Labor-Management Group were also part of the Business Roundtable, a lobbying organization set up in 1972 to counter what executives regarded as overly powerful unions and a hostile regulatory climate. No less than the head of the Roundtable, DuPont's Irving Shapiro, was also part of Dunlop's group. That meant that even as Dunlop was presiding over collaborative talks with labor and business leaders, those same corporate chiefs were at work trying to prevent the unions from realizing legislative gains from their strong showing in the election that might "tip the balance in industrial relations," as A.H. Raskin, the *New York Times*' resident labor expert described it.[12]

Relations between the AFL-CIO and the Carter Administration got off to a rocky start and never really recovered. George Meany was displeased with Carter's choice for secretary of labor, Dunlop's friend Ray Marshall; Meany and others had been pushing for Dunlop himself to be reappointed. And by the time the AFL-CIO unveiled its legislative agenda, there were growing signs that the political climate was tilting against labor. The labor group was also deeply unhappy with the Carter Administration's stimulus package, unveiled in January of 1977, which labor leaders saw as both too small, and focused on the wrong thing: tax cuts rather than job creation. But that battle, which the AFL-CIO lost, was a mere precursor to the war over a proposed minimum wage increase. While the labor organization was pushing for a substantial raise, from $2.30 to $3.00 per hour, the Carter Administration proposed a hike of just twenty cents. George Meany responded with outrage, stating that such a meager increase was a "bitter disappointment to everyone who looked to this administration for economic justice for the poor."[13]

While a compromise increased the minimum wage to $2.65, even a partial victory didn't assuage Meany, Kirkland and other labor leaders, who felt disrespected by the new administration. Political historian Taylor Dark argues that Meany and his fellow union leaders were not entirely wrong about this. In addition to the rising influence of the conservative right and the Business Roundtable, President Carter also had a governing philosophy that was profoundly at odds with the world in which Dunlop and the unions operated. Writes Dark: "[Carter] had developed a worldview that stressed the need for virtuous leaders to promote the public interest against the parochial demands of self-serving interest groups."[14] Such a characterization, Dark notes, was completely at odds with how labor leaders saw themselves. "To the union leaders, their organizations were not 'special interest groups' undermining the public good, but legitimate representative bodies that deserved to be consulted—not merely out of politeness or political expediency, but exactly because of their genuinely representational character."[15]

SMILES AND CLASS WAR

In the spring of 1977, the AFL-CIO made yet another attempt to get situs picketing legislation through Congress. With the backing of President Carter and Secretary of Labor Marshall, labor leaders and their lobbyists on Capitol Hill were optimistic that they could muster enough support this time to see the bill passed. But in the two years since House members had last taken up the issue, political and geographic fault lines had widened. Not only did Republicans from the northern states fail to back the bill this time around, there was increased opposition from southern Democrats as well. In a telling omen of what was to come, every Democrat from Alabama, Arkansas, Georgia, Mississippi and North Carolina voted against the picketing bill, while northern Democrats supported it.[16]

But the real showdown came over a labor-backed package of proposed reforms to the National Labor Relations Act. The hope of the AFL-CIO and the bill's other supporters was that by deterring violations of the NLRA, the measure would make it easier for unorganized workers to join unions, thus stemming a decline in numbers that was getting hard to ignore. In order to win passage, the bill's backers had watered it down considerably. Stripped from the legislation were the provisions that Raskin described for the *Times* as being "most likely to stir fierce doctrinal struggle with management and conservative elements in Congress."[17] Gone was a call for a repeal of section 14(b) of the Taft-Hartley Act, which allowed states to establish right to work laws. Gone too was the demand for majority "card check" in union elections.

The new, more moderate approach, crafted by labor leaders and lobbyists in close consultation with Carter Administration officials and Democratic leadership, reflected the AFL-CIO's pragmatism under Meany, wrote Raskin. "One of the foundation stones for George Meany's many successes in quarter century as chief lobbyist for organized labor at the White House and on Capitol Hill is his firm belief that "'ideology is baloney.'"[18] This time around, Meany and his lieutenants were counting on a strategy of caution—steering clear of ideological landmines—coupled with the political influence labor had vis a vis the Labor-Management Group, to see labor law reform through Congress and avoid the embarrassing defeat of situs the previous year.

Labor's public relations strategy will feel instantly familiar to observers of the 2009 legislative battle over the Employee Free Choice Act. The AFL-CIO brought individual workers to Washington to make the case for why labor law reform was desperately needed—like 77-year-old Thelma Swann, whose South Carolina textile mill was closed by Deering Milliken after she and her co-workers formed a union. The workers' case had made it all the way to the Supreme Court, which had ruled in their favor. But after 21 years, Swann had never received the back pay she was owed. "There has been untold suffering," Swann said in her Congressional testimony.

But the stories of Swann and others proved to be no match for the wall of opposition from the business lobby, which successfully painted the watered-down reform package as a naked power grab by union bosses. The proposed overhaul was "anti-business," argued the CEO of the Associated General Contractors, James Sprouse, noting that his organization planned to join with "the general business community in vigorously opposing this legislation."[19]

While the bill made it through the House of Representatives with relative ease, it met with near hostility on the Senate floor, where debate didn't begin until May of 1978. Behind the intense opposition was a PR offensive that put even the earlier anti-situs campaign to shame. Owners of small businesses deluged senators with letters and phone calls. The National Right to Work Committee alone sent senators 4 million pieces of mail. Organizations representing large corporations soon joined the fray, creating enough resistance that Senate opponents of the bill, namely Richard Lugar and Orrin Hatch, could filibuster it. Labor law reform officially died on June 15, 1978, crushed by a newly energized and organized business lobby, exemplified by the Business Roundtable. As Mike Davis notes, the emergence of the Roundtable represented a "quantum leap" in the business lobby's level of organization. Suddenly 160 of the largest companies in the US were united within a single association, able to agitate on behalf of their own policy priorities, and against those they regarded as anti-business. [20]

"With tactical initiative in the economy and Congress slipping to corporations, there was simply no important constraint to induce them to take the corporatist ideas of Dunlop or the AFL-CIO seriously," writes Davis.[21] Despite having a Congress two-thirds controlled by Democrats, the labor movement had been thoroughly outmaneuvered by some of the same companies that sat across the table from them as part of the Labor-Management Group. The contradictory role played by the presidents of such companies as General Electric and DuPont was described by labor leaders Douglas Fraser of the UAW and Lane Kirkland as "smiles and class war."[22]

Fraser had no illusions about what had happened. A month after labor law reform succumbed to a Senate filibuster, he submitted his letter of resignation to the Labor-Management Group. He had the highest regard for John Dunlop and his colleagues on the labor side, wrote Fraser, and respected, as individuals, those who were representing the corporate elite, but he no longer believed it was in the interest of the UAW or its members to participate.

> Attractive as the personalities may be, we all sit in a representative capacity. I have concluded that participation in these meetings is no longer useful to me or to the 1.5 million workers I represent as president of the UAW. I believe leaders of the business community, with few exceptions, have chosen to wage a one-sided class war today in this country—a war against working people, the unemployed, the poor, the minorities, the very young and the very old, and even many in the middle class of our society. The leaders of industry, commerce and finance in the United States have broken and discarded the fragile, unwritten compact previously existing during a past period of growth and progress.[23]

Fraser's letter excoriated the members of the Labor-Management Group, not just for the general shift away from cooperation with labor and towards confrontation, but for their specific actions during the battle over labor law reform. While some of the corporate chiefs had pressed the Business Roundtable to remain neutral on the issue, they lost, meaning that their companies proceeded to bankroll the multi-million-dollar lobbying and public relations offensive against the bill. The resulting fight by the business community against the labor law reform bill, wrote Fraser, "stands as the most vicious, unfair attack upon the labor movement in more than 30 years."[24]

Nor was Fraser being particularly hyperbolic. The stepped-up lobbying by business interests, the highly organized PR strategy, and the coordinated targeting of congressmen in their home districts, was markedly different than how industry had operated in the past. In fact, it looked a lot like labor's style of lobbying, only more effective. Campaign contributions were way up as well. As Dark notes, between 1972 and 1978, campaign expenditures from business PACS increased from $8 million to $39 million, far outpacing union spending during the same time period.[25] One didn't have to look far to "discern a demand by business for docile government and unrestrained corporate individualism," that Fraser warned about.[26]

TAKING THE LONG VIEW

Political analysts at the time interpreted Fraser's fiery resignation as a sign that the power balance in industrial relations was shifting back towards employers and away from thirty years of post-war peace. "Autoworker Pullout Signals Labor Strife," was the headline of one *Washington Post* story, whose author, Frank Swoboda, lamented the end of "the last major forum left for labor and management leaders to meet privately to discuss common problems."[27] Raskin argued in the *Times* that the *rapproachement* between labor and industry obscured the extent to which unions had become dependent upon management to do their recruiting for them via union shop contracts. Management had become "the principal recruiting agenda for a labor movement that had run out of steam." And it was the end of that arrangement that labor leaders were most galled by, wrote Raskin.[28]

Meany and Kirkland resigned soon after Fraser. The Labor-Management Group was dead and with it, seemingly, the post-war consensus in labor management relations. But did John Dunlop share that perspective? Did he see corporate America's shift towards confrontation as a threat to the concept of countervailing power—organized businesses, organized workers, government serving as a broker between them—that he believed was so essential to a stable society? In his 1984 book on dispute resolution, Dunlop gives a clue into his thinking at the time. He comments that despite the rising public acrimony in the fall of 1978, controversial matters had not been under discussion in the group. "In retrospect, this detachment may have been a mistake."[29]

Dunlop gave no public indication that his fundamental view of labor and business having mutually beneficial interests had been shaken, or that he'd lost faith in the concept of a labor/management forum as the best setting to deal with big, complex problems. While the Labor-Management Group ceased to reconvene after the UAW's pullout, it would survive in other iterations, culminating ultimately in Dunlop's next high-profile exercise in collaboration: the Clinton-era Dunlop Commission. As Dunlop told Richard Bartels in a 1982 interview for the economics magazine *Challenge*: "It is important in a democratic society for labor and management to be able to know each other, to talk with each other about broad issues of national and international economics and related policies."[30]

But what of the role that business leaders who were part of the Labor-Management Group played in working to undercut labor law reform? Did Dunlop see the dual "hats" of members like DuPont's Irving Shapiro, who also headed up the Business Roundtable, as undermining the glue of self-interest upon which the collaborative instrument depended? In *Dispute Resolution,* Dunlop noted that the management members of the group who were also leaders of the Business Round Table, namely Reginald Jones, Shapiro and Thomas Murphy, were outvoted when they recommended that their organization take no official position on labor-law reform.[31] Meanwhile Dunlop's faith that the cooperative venture could issue policy recommendations on the pressing economic issues of the day was undiminished. Even as the political climate grew more acrimonious, the Labor-Management Group and its assorted staff members continued to produce high-level and far-reaching position papers on inflation as well as various aspects of the Carter Administration's energy policy.

While Dunlop no doubt understood Fraser's reasons for leaving the Labor-Management Group, it is important to note that labor law reform per se was never within the purview of the committee. Expanding the committee's focus beyond what it was originally set up to do would have violated a basic tenet of Dunlop's approach. There was another reason why the group was not an appropriate setting for labor to make its case for reforming the nation's labor laws: the management side was divided between companies with unionized workforces and those without. Any legal change that would have made organizing workers easier would almost certainly have affected the group's non-union participants: DuPont, Sears, Roebuck, Mobil and Citicorp. Meany and his colleagues seemed to acknowledge as much in a *New York Times* news analysis piece that ran in the summer of 1977 about labor's new spirit of cooperation.[32]

In his 1982 interview, Dunlop lamented a political atmosphere "so charged with hostility that . . . resolution is less easily achieved."[33] Fraser's resignation and the subsequent breakup of the Labor-Management Group had presaged much worse to come. And yet Dunlop not only held onto his belief that a "consultative, cooperative process" was essential to resolving complex economic and political problem, he refused to see the decline in labor's fortunes as indicative of some tectonic shift. While his colleagues at the AFL-CIO were sounding ominous warnings of corporate America's "holy war" against workers and the unions that represented them, Dunlop necessarily took a longer view of what was happening. His perspective was that of the historian, interpreting political developments against the backdrop of the whole sweep of industrial relations. "I'm not worried about people who recognize they have different interests, and indeed, labor and management inherently do," Dunlop told Bartel. "In our kind of society you have to recognize conflicting interests among many different groups and still find workable arrangements."[34]

Dunlop regarded the Labor-Management Group as one of his great accomplishments. It was organized and reorganized, recalled Dunlop, "out of the ashes of the fiery conflict" between business and labor over labor law reform in 1978. But even as civil conversations with labor leaders and corporate executive continued, the economy was further deteriorating, the political climate growing increasingly hostile. While Ronald Reagan wouldn't assume the presidency for three more years, 1978 represented, in many ways, the commencement of "Reaganomics." Congress largely embraced the agenda of the Business Roundtable, including freezing social spending, deregulating major industries and moving to higher interest rates. Signs that the post-war social contract was fraying were getting harder to ignore.

Two years after Meany and Kirkland resigned from the Labor-Management Group, some of its remaining corporate members, notably GE's Reginald Jones, Dupont's Irving Shapiro and GM's Thomas Murphy persuaded Kirkland to rejoin. Kirkland, who by this time had replaced Meany as the head of the AFL-CIO, served as a co-chairman of the organization alongside the CEO of Exxon, Clifton Garvin. Garvin, meanwhile, was also the head of the Business Roundtable. In its statement of purpose, the new entity identified its focus as "the area of economic policy in which its collective experience is based." The statement referenced the increasingly heated nature of the political debate over labor-management relations: "It is destructive to society and to business and organized labor if, in our legitimate adversarial roles, we question the right of our institutions to exist and perform their legitimate functions."[35]

But the fracture lines that had been exposed between labor and industry during the battle over labor law reform were widening. Even as the sides were meeting once again to discuss their common interests, Exxon was embarking on a multi-billion dollar oil shale project in the Rocky Mountains. It used nonunion labor.[36]

NOTES

1. John T. Dunlop, personal diary, April 6, 1975–February 26, 1976, sec.17, 81.
2. Ibid.
3. Diary, sec. 18, 12.
4. Diary, sec. 10, 31.
5. John T. Dunlop, *Dispute Resolution: Negotiation and Consensus Building*, (Dover, MA: Auburn House Publishing, 1984), 252.
6. Diary, sec. 8, 2.
7. Ibid.
8. Diary, sec. 8, 3.
9. *Dispute Resolution*, p. 254.

10. Leonard Silk, “Inflation Fighters Tripartite Forum,” *New York Times,* July 4th, 1977.

11. Mike Davis, *Prisoners of the American Dream: Politics and Economy in the History of the US Working Class*, (New York: Verso, 1986), 135.

12. A.H. Raskin “Concessions in Labor’s Pragmatic Stance,” *The New York Times*, June 15, 1977.

13. Cited in Taylor Dark, *Unions and the Democrats: an Enduring Alliance*, (Ithaca, NY: ILR Press, 1999), 106.

14. Ibid., 105.

15. Ibid.

16. Philip Shabecoff, “House Rejects Bill on Picketing Sites by Building Unions,” *New York Times,* March 23, 1977.

17. A.H. Raskin, “Concessions in Labor’s Pragmatic Stance.”

18. Ibid.

19. Philip Shabecoff, “Washington and Business,” *New York Times,* July 21, 1977.

20. Davis, 135.

21. Ibid.

22. Ibid.

23. Doug Fraser’s Resignation Letter from the Labor-Management Group, *Daily Labor Report*, no. 139, July 17, 1978.

24. Ibid.

25. Dark, p. 112.

26. Fraser Resignation Letter.

27. Frank Swoboda, “Autoworker Pullout Signals Labor Strife,” *Washington Post*, July 21, 1978.

28. “Big Labor Strives to Break Out of Its Rut,” *Fortune*, August 27, 1979, 33.

29. *Dispute Resolution*, p. 256.

30. John Dunlop and Richard Bartel, “Working Towards Consensus,” *Challenge*, 25, no. 3 (July/August 1982): 32.

31. *Dispute Resolution*, p. 256.

32. A.H. Raskin, “Concessions in Labor’s Pragmatic Stance.”

33. Dunlop and Bartel, p. 34.

34. Ibid.

35. Statement of Purpose, Labor-Management Group, 1981, cited in Dunlop, *Dispute Resolution*, p. 257.

36. Thomas Byrd Edsall, *The New Politics of Inequality*, (New York: W.W. Norton, 1985), 186.

Chapter Six

Back to the Future of Work

"President Clinton has asked me to head up this damn committee on the future of labor and management relations."[1] That's how Dunlop described to his colleagues the summons he'd received to head up the Commission on the Future of Worker-Management Relations, a far-reaching effort to examine labor-management cooperation, employee participation in the workplace and dispute resolution in American workplaces. By the time he was tapped by Clinton's secretary of labor, Robert Reich, to chair the commission, Dunlop was 80 years old, and an emeritus professor at Harvard.

Dunlop had spent the long years of the Reagan administration largely working outside of government. The Clinton appointment would be his first official administrative post since the Carter-era Labor-Management Group. Dunlop spent much of that time pursuing what he described as institutional innovations at Harvard, an institution that as he noted, was "not readily changed."[2] He'd helped to develop a new program of study in Business and Economics, a Joint Center for Housing, and a new division of Health Policy, all of which reflected his own deep belief in the need for interdisciplinary and inter-institutional approaches. Then there was his dispute resolution and problem-solving work in a dizzying array of industries: construction, agriculture, textiles, health care, and at Harvard itself, where Dunlop negotiated the first contract between the university and the new union of clerical and technical workers. When he received the request from the Clinton administration, Dunlop was in the midst of a top-to-bottom investigation into the American textile industry, aimed at helping it survive the ravages of global competition.[3]

As his Harvard colleague Quinn Mills observes, Dunlop's shift from a high-level political role in the 1970's to sector-specific projects through the 1980's was itself a reflection of the changing relationship between labor, business and government. Explains Mills: "He still had access to the unions and potential access to the employers, but without access to the government, he couldn't do as much."[4] Dunlop's fear that his departure as secretary of labor in 1976 would leave no one in the highest ranks of government who understood unions or collective bargaining had been more than borne out in the ensuing decade and a half. Not only had labor law reform failed in one administration after another, but the rights of workers were increasingly under siege.

The activist orientation of US business interests that succeeded in quashing labor law reform in 1978 took further flight during the era of Reagan. The economy, meanwhile, was mired in a deep recession, triggered in large part by the actions of Federal Reserve chair Paul Volker, who was determined to conquer inflation once and for all. There were other forces at work too. US markets were suddenly and dramatically opened to foreign competition, while domestic companies increasingly competed on a global stage. The era of wage stability and shared prosperity appeared to be over, replaced by wage concessions and two-tiered labor agreements, with newly hired workers often earning far less than their predecessors. Reagan himself signaled the changing times in 1981 with his dramatic firing of the PATCO workers.

But did these setbacks for labor represent an historical blip or were they representative of deeper, structural changes to the economy? While debate would rage among academics, including Dunlop, who believed the reports of labor's demise to be greatly exaggerated, the economic recovery of the 1980's, followed by the boom times of the 1990's, provided an answer. Labor's fortunes did not improve. There was no return to the bargaining power that unions had enjoyed after World War II, stemming as it did from their sheer numbers and their ability to threaten strikes. As manufacturing jobs fled the unionized North for the non-union Sun Belt states, union power ebbed. The decline of industrial unions also upended the tradition of pattern bargaining, in which wage and benefit agreements reached by unions and employers would then spread across the economy to include nonunion workers.

The election of Bill Clinton in 1992 represented a long-awaited opportunity to reverse this tide. With Democrats in control of Congress, unions immediately began pushing for legislation that would end the permanent replacement of striking workers, a practice that had greatly eroded the potency of the strike as a weapon. The bill, far narrower in scope than the labor law reform sought by unions in 1977, met the same fate as its predecessor, passing the House before succumbing to a Senate filibuster. A more promising effort to finally restore balance to the nation's shredded labor laws came at the behest of the new president himself. In an effort to appease labor leaders who strongly opposed his trade policies, Clinton established a commission to study the state of US labor law and make recommendations to

Congress. The body, established in the spring of 1993, was officially known as the Commission on the Future of Worker-Management Relations. But even its members, a mix of academics, government officials, labor leaders and corporate executives, rarely referred to it by that title. Instead it was known by the name of its chair: the Dunlop Commission.

For Dunlop, the commission represented a major opportunity, not just to return to Washington, but to head up a national labor-management commission of the sort that he'd put so much stock in throughout his long career. "I thought at the time, and still do, that this new commission represented a unique opportunity that doesn't come along very often," Dunlop told interviewer Bruce Kaufman in 2002.[5] The scope of the new commission's work was also broader than the handful of previous convenings on industrial relations, beginning with the US Commission on Industrial Relations, convened from 1913–1915. While other commissions had followed, including the La Follette Committee's investigation of employer practices in the 1950's and the McClelland Committee, which looked into union corruption in the 1950's, these were fairly specific in nature. "There have been more focused and detailed inquiries," Dunlop wrote in a 1996 paper, "But the federal government has seldom undertaken so comprehensive a review of worker-management relations and the American workplace."[6]

The group was instructed to look at three question, which Dunlop summed up as: 1) What (if any) new methods or institutions should be encouraged, or required, to enhance workplace productivity through labor-management cooperation and employee participation? 2) What (if any) changes should be made in the present legal framework and practices of collective bargaining to enhance cooperative behavior, improve productivity, and reduce conflict and delay? 3) What, if anything, should be done to increase the extent to which workplace problems are directly resolved by the parties themselves, rather than through recourse to state and federal courts and government?[7]

The scope of the questions meant going well beyond previous attempts to shore up the country's increasingly tattered labor laws and thinking instead about what the American workplace *could* look like. "The issues are a lot broader now than simply labor and management," Dunlop told the *Washington Post's* Frank Swoboda, as the commission was beginning its work.[8] As he explained, the new body's focus would extend to revisiting the question of how the federal government regulated the workplace and investigating whether there might not be a better way to carry out that work.

But from its inception the Dunlop Commission's very mission—even its existence—was fraught. Some labor advocates, including Tom Kochan, a professor of industrial relations at MIT who would serve as a member of the Commission, felt very strongly that the dawn of the new Clinton Administration represented an all-too-rare opportunity for significant labor policy reform. "Whatever you do, don't set up some blue-ribbon commission to search for consensus for a new policy," wrote Kochan in a cautionary memo to Clinton's Secretary of Labor, Robert Reich. "There is no deal to be made between labor and management on this."[9] Internal divisions and ideological differences, Kochan argued, would prevent both sides from being bold. The AFL-CIO was pushing hard for just such a body, however, and in the end the labor group would win out. The result was an effort to both document the problems of the existing structure of labor law and explore the possibilities of an entirely new framework for worker/management relations.

FACT FINDING

The Future of Worker-Management Relations was officially announced by Secretary of Labor Robert Reich and Secretary of Commerce Ron Brown on March 24, 1993. Its ten members were an impressive bunch, with three former Secretaries of Labor—John Dunlop, Bill Usery and Ray Marshall—professors from Stanford, Harvard, MIT and the University of Wisconsin; the UAW's former chief, Doug Fraser; and two corporate CEO's, Paul Allaire of Xerox and Kathryn Turner of Standard Technology, representing the small business community. The sheer breadth of the commission's undertaking is conveyed in the numbers. In the 20 months of its existence, the commission conducted 21 public hearings, in Washington D.C., as well as in six other cities. Testimony was collected from 411 witnesses, and more than 160 other statements were entered into the public record. The commission also solicited special studies on the views of employers and unions regarding particular workplace regulations, and on the attitudes of workers towards workplace participation and union representation.[10]

The commission's dual focus upon present-day problems and future solutions was represented in the very structure of the undertaking, namely the decision to produce two separate reports. The fact-finding volume was followed by a final report: 115 pages of recommendations for modernizing American labor and employment law and administration for the future. "I thought it was important to first get consensus on the basic issues and problems, and then try to go back and come up with solutions that people could support," Dunlop explained.[11] The lengthy fact-gathering process was also intended to serve another purpose. By establishing that there was indeed a crisis, and documenting trends such as stagnant wages, inequality, global competition and high unemployment for unskilled workers, the commission could then make the case for particular solutions.

Just as the commission paid homage to the rare tradition of labor/management problem solving bodies in US history, it was also acting upon a lesson from previous such efforts. The only fundamental changes in labor/management law in US history had come during times of great crisis. The LaFollette Committee investigations in the 1930's, for example, had influenced key provisions of the National Labor Relations Act. Six decades later, the members of the Clinton-era commission were hoping that a year of fact finding, summed up in a report released in June of 1994, would provide a definitive account of the state of the American workplace, making clear that action was needed. Among the body's key findings: 1) The process for choosing workplace representation was no longer working well. It took too long, and had become both adversarial and legalistic, with the end result that workers who wanted union representation were too often denied it; 2) The illegal dismissal of workers who tried to organize unions was on the rise, while the number of first contracts that were successfully negotiated after workers unionized was on the decline; 3) Disputes between workers and management were increasingly likely to end up in court; 4) Employee participation in workplace decision making was also on the increase, especially at so-called "high-production" companies.

As the report made clear, these findings were intertwined, often in complicated ways. Already a key tension in the commission's approach was making itself felt: "complicated" and "intertwined" are different from "crisis"; if the group meant to provide a roadmap, it wasn't at all clear what the destination should be. Take the issue of employee decision making, for example. For the AFL-CIO, which had pushed hard for the commission, the findings about the rise in illegal dismissals and the demand for worker voice were a clear indication of the need to make union organizing easier. But some of the worker/management teams cited by the commission as models were at companies with no unions.

Commission member Doug Fraser, the former UAW president who'd resigned from Dunlop's previous Labor-Management Group with such fireworks, foreshadowed the difficulty that was to come with his response to the fact-finding report. Worker/management teams were fine, said Fraser, as long as the workers had a union. "If you are going to have true labor-management cooperation, then you have to have an equal partnership, and that requires unions to protect workers," said Fraser.[12] The response from corporate leaders was similarly lukewarm. Jeffrey McGuiness, head of the pro-employer Labor Policy Association, said that he doubted that the business community would be supportive of making it easier for unions to organize, and questioned whether a brokered deal responding to the myriad employment issues raised by the Commission was even possible.[13]

In December of 1994, the Dunlop Commission released its final report, wrapping up more than 20 months of work and countless hours spent taking testimony from labor groups and business leaders, advocacy organizations, labor law experts and individual workers. The timing could not have been worse. By the time the group went public with its recommendations, the balance of power in Washington had shifted dramatically. The GOP had swept control of both houses of Congress under the leadership of a conservative firebrand from Georgia named Newt Gingrich. The window for reforming labor law had just slammed shut. In a climate that would turn ever more hostile, there was virtually no place for the commission's thoughtful, nuanced proposals for making workplace relations between labor and management less adversarial.

Yet what stands out more than two decades after the body concluded its work is both the enormity of the challenge Dunlop and his fellow commission members took on and the spirit with which they took on that challenge. As the fact-finding report documented, the American workplace had undergone dramatic changes such that the existing institutions and regulations were outmoded, even counterproductive. More than just updates or tinkering around the edges would be needed to make an out-of-date system function in today's workplaces, whether they were industrial factories struggling to compete in a global era or part of the fast-growing high-tech sector. The commission was proposing new systems and regulations, indeed a whole new way of thinking about the workplace and how workers and management might relate.

The road map foreshadowed in the fact-finding report had led the commission in two distinct directions. The first was an overhaul of labor law reform. Among the proposed changes: extending legal safeguards to the rapidly expanding population of contingent workers; speeding up union elections; cracking down on employers who violated labor law and retaliated against employees who sought to organize unions; and involving tripartite bodies in order to ease the process of negotiating first contracts. The commission also suggested various ways to simplify federal regulations that worked against the swift resolution of disputes, including the adoption of alternative dispute resolution. But much of the group's focus was on the "future" in the body's official title, including envisioning ways that management and workers could team up to solve workplace problems. As the report stated: "Taken together, these recommendations give workers and managers the tools and flexibility to do what they say they want to do and are capable of doing to improve workplace performance. We recommend flexibility in employee participation while ensuring respect for workers' rights to choose unions, if desired."[14]

DISINTEGRATION

In John Dunlop's long and storied career, the Clinton-era Commission that bore his name was one of his few real failures. Falling well far short of its declared aims and goals, the body's work has largely been relegated to a footnote in the history of failed attempts to reform the nation's labor laws. And while Dunlop would continue to push for the use of alternative dispute resolution and joint labor/management councils for problem solving, the commission itself had little impact. The consensus among analysts of the period is that the Dunlop Commission was a victim of the dramatic shift in political tides; the combination of poor timing, bad luck and politics meant its proposals were dead on arrival. But the enterprise was beset from the start by tensions between the demands of a labor movement that was desperate to stem years of decline, and the Clinton Administration, which was far more interested in the question of how to improve American economic competitiveness, whether or not the answer included unions at all. In the end, the commission's attempt to split the difference would appease neither the unions or employers. Meanwhile Dunlop's trademark approach of bringing together leaders from labor and business and hashing out differences, honed over so many years and in a wide array of forums, was largely unsuccessful in this instance.

What made this endeavor different than others in which Dunlop had been involved? For one, Dunlop himself was constrained by a structure that wasn't of his choice or his making. By this point in his career, he had settled on a particular way of doing business, as he liked to say. His approach typically began with getting the right people in the room, then determining the rules of engagement. By the time he was tapped to head up the Clinton effort, however, key decisions had already been made, down to who would serve as his executive assistant. "One of the things John was so good at was picking people and mentoring them and thinking about what kind of person he needed," recalls Dunlop protégé David Weil.[15]

While Dunlop had worked with both public and private entities over the years, he far preferred a closed-door setting for getting the right people together and mediating settlements. In his interview with Richard Bartel in 1982, he went so far as to argue that "anyone who knows the first thing about negotiations knows that no serious negotiations can ever take place in public."[16] But the private arrangements he preferred were all but impossible a decade later. The Federal Advisory Committee Act or FACA rules that he'd railed against back beginning in his days overseeing the Cost of Living Council had only grown more restrictive since then. As for the after-hours "sessions" he was fond of holding with government officials and labor and business leaders, the highly public nature of the Dunlop Commission was a world away from the watering holes Dunlop favored. "He'd have a string of people coming through and they'd get their 20 minutes with John over a scotch to figure things out," says Weil. "He simply couldn't do that in the Dunlop Commission setting."[17]

The highly public nature of the Dunlop Commission's work went against another of Dunlop's deeply held tenets: that publicity was an enemy of serious negotiating. If working behind closed doors better enabled him to call upon his powers of persuasion, it also kept labor and business leaders from engaging in what Dunlop referred to disparagingly as "speechmaking." But with so much of the commission's business conducted in the open, speechmaking was inevitably part of the process. Secretary of Labor Robert Reich, for example, who'd convened the body and was its nominal head, was also a high-profile media figure who delighted in engaging in spirited combat with the Clinton administration's adversaries. Unlike Dunlop, Reich was perfectly at ease in the new era of cable TV politics. It was another small but key sign that the world in which Dunlop had operated so effectively and for so long had changed.

Communications styles and even staffing picks were small ball when compared to the deep divide between the commission's labor constituents and its "future-focused" members. The dispute emerged even before the body went public with its recommendations. In its fact-finding report, the commission pointed to labor/management partnerships as a hallmark of highly performing workplaces. As the report noted, the existence of such partnerships over a sustained period of time seemed to pay off in higher productivity, and yet there were relatively few examples of such teams in the American workplace. The solution, argued the commission in its final report, was to relax the section of the National Labor Relations Act that prohibited employer-dominated labor organizations in order to allow quality circles and other employer participation groups to flourish.

The recommendation neatly encapsulated the commission's challenge to update labor law as a means of making American workplaces more competitive. The problem was that the unions, at whose urging the Clinton had convened the panel, disagreed with this approach. Former UAW chief Doug Fraser refused to endorse the final report, arguing that: "[e]mployer-dominated representation is undemocratic regardless of the particular subjects with which the employer-controlled representative deals."[18] Fraser's strong objection only solidified the complaints he'd raised during the fact-finding process: that a partnership between labor and management could not be equal unless workers had a truly independent voice and the guaranteed protections of a union.

Fraser was far from a lone voice. AFL-CIO Secretary-Treasurer Tom Donahue was extremely unhappy with what he recalls as "this company union idea."[19] An ally of Dunlop's for many years—Donahue had worked closely with Dunlop to set up the labor/management forum for farmworkers, growers and major food processors described in the next chapter—the labor leader now found himself at odds with his long-time friend. He recalls talking to Dunlop again and again while the commission was meeting, conversations that often turned heated. Dunlop would make the case for what he saw as a limited change to section 8(a)(2) of the NLRA, clarifying employee involvement in workplaces without unions. "'This is the way to rebuild the labor movement," Donahue recalls Dunlop saying. Donahue would cite history: the experiences that unions had had at the turn of the century when company-created unions were a staple of the American workplace. "All of our unions have had bad experiences with that," was Donahue's standard response. "It's not going to fly."[20]

Donahue says that he thinks that Dunlop believed that the unions could be swayed to support the proposal. As the commission wrapped up its work and the final report was being prepared, Donahue was as firm as ever. The AFL-CIO would not get behind the commission's recommendations and was prepared to denounce them. It is a period of time that Donahue looks back upon with regret. While the commission's recommendations went nowhere, and the NLRA's prohibition against management domination of unions remains on the books today, his long friendship with Dunlop didn't survive the acrimony over labor law reform. "John was absolutely convinced that he was right," recalls Donahue. "It became a very bitter period of time."[21]

In his 2002 interview, Dunlop seemed to echo the AFL-CIO's concerns, maintaining that while there could be a place for workplace committees in nonunion settings to address specific issues, such as health and safety, anything involving what he terms "negotiat[ing] over things" should be off limits. "When it comes to any kind of negotiation, I think it is very important that the employees be able to choose their own representatives, rather than have them chosen by management. I also think there is a real possibility that these committees end up in many cases as another means to subvert genuine collective bargaining," warned Dunlop.[22] While several commission members had made the case that it was time for the US to adapt European-style work councils, Dunlop left no doubt as to his feelings on the issue. Since there seemed to be no real demand for works councils, to consider them was to engage in intellectual speculation. "And I am *particularly* hostile to talking about changing labor policy based on intellectual speculation," he added with emphasis.[23]

The corporate titans with whom Dunlop had had close relationships, like GE's Reginald Jones, were now largely gone, and a changing of the guard was well underway. Jones' successor at GE was Jack Welch, who was known by the unionized workers at the company as "Neutron Jack" for his "nuclear" approach to labor management. And it wasn't just the guard that was changing but the entire structure of the corporate world. As industrial relations scholar and commission member Tom Kochan points out, the new businesses that were being created during this period were overwhelmingly nonunion and determined to stay that way. The high-tech industry that was emerging as a such a force had virtually no unions, and manufacturing appeared to be moving in that direction. With that historical change came an enormous shift in influence. "Power shifted from the old-line industries and from the old-line industrial relations professionals in those industries to non-union firms and to HR executives who had no allegiance to or experience with John Dunlop or his generation," says Kochan.[24] And that meant that getting the "right people" in the room, something that was at the very heart of Dunlop's approach, simply wasn't possible any more. The business leaders who held increasing sway didn't see any particular reason to engage.

Kochan has long maintained that the Dunlop Commission was the wrong instrument to achieve a change in labor policy. He'd argued from the first days of the Clinton administration that the window to enact a new labor policy was too brief to spend time studying the issue. In his view, the administration erred by not identifying key principles that were in keeping with Clinton's vision for a new economy, developing a legislative program, and pushing hard to get it enacted. But Kochan also believes that Dunlop was simply the wrong person to head up the commission. "John was this great problem solver, but the world had changed around him in ways that the skill set he had no longer fit the range of actors that needed to be brought together," says Kochan. "There was no deal, and there still is no deal."[25]

Much of the 20 months of the commission's work was spent in efforts to convince Dunlop that the system of industrial relations that he'd spent his life's work immersed in had changed beyond recognition, says Kochan. While the two of them were often at odds during this period—they were also on opposite sides of a long-running academic debate over the magnitude of the shift in industrial relations—they struck up a friendship. During the long working sessions on what would become the commission's final report, Dunlop would share his concern that the principles of fair, effective and efficient labor relations were eroding as management increasingly refused to engage with labor. Recalls Kochan: "He said a couple of time, 'I've never seen things as bad as they are now.' It really bothered him, and I understand it, because he helped to build that industrial relations system."[26]

ADMINISTRATIVE ACTIONS

"The elections of 1994 antedated the Commission's recommendations, and our legislative proposals would not be and were not received with favor by the majority of the November 1994 elected Congress." Dunlop made this dispassionate assessment in an unpublished paper he delivered to a gathering of dispute resolution experts two years after the "Republican Revolution."[27] Yet even as the dramatic political shift made legislative action impossible, Dunlop saw important openings regarding commission recommendations that required only administrative actions. The section of the final report that was specific to the railroad and airline industries, for example, laid out a series of suggestions, based on input from labor and management representatives, for making collective bargaining operate more effectively. Working with Bill Usery, who had replaced him as secretary of labor in the Ford administration, Dunlop moved to quickly implement the outlined procedures, including bipartite meetings and conferences between the various parties aimed at addressing an overarching question: what could be done to make negotiations in these industries less contentious?

The commission identified major problems with the union election process, specifically the proportion of elections that failed to produce a first collective bargaining agreement, or resulted in unreasonably lengthy negotiation periods. And while the proposed legislative remedy had been decisively rejected by management organizations, the commission encouraged both the National Labor Relations Board and the Federal Mediation and Conciliation Service to take steps to remedy these problems at the administrative level. As Dunlop noted in his 1996 assessment, these efforts found at least some success. One significant change: a mediator was assigned to assist with a first collective bargaining agreement as soon as new unions were certified. The commission had also suggested that representatives of the relevant agencies prepare an annual report in order to better understand both the scope and the nature of failures to reach agreement in first contracts. "More effective mediation can reduce their numbers and the time required," wrote Dunlop.[28]

Dunlop devoted particular attention and energy to furthering the use of alternative dispute resolution in employment law disputes. The commission's fact-finding report had identified the rapid growth in federal court cases involving employment law as major problem. The sheer volume of cases was overwhelming the system, as surging demand met agencies crippled by budget cuts. The result was a broken system, characterized by backlogs and delays in which parties could wait years to have their cases heard. As Dunlop saw it, such disfunction also represented a major opportunity to push for the use of alternative dispute resolution in employment law disputes. The sudden rise of employer-imposed arbitration systems gave the cause an added urgency. By the time the Dunlop Commission convened, more than 100 employers had established these, and by some predictions, half of all employees in the country would be required to arbitrate discrimination claims within the decade.[29]

In the summer of 1994, Dunlop called upon his long-time Harvard colleague and fellow mediator Arnold Zack to assist with the project of following through on the commission's recommendations regarding "fair, expeditious and inexpensive resolution of workplace statutory disputes." [30] The Harvard Law School professor mused to Dunlop that there ought to be a way to apply the principles of the labor management dispute resolution process, with its expectation of negotiated fairness, to nonunion settings. Dunlop responded in his "true academic style," recalls Zack, "taunt[ing] me into trying to write a proposal for assuring such protections."[31]

What would come to be known as the Due Process Protocols was a response to both the emergence of employer-imposed arbitration and the glaring need for a better employment dispute resolution system. Zack responded to Dunlop's challenge by poring over collective bargaining agreements, identifying the essential elements of procedural fairness. "You're getting these disputes, employers have got to create these structures to resolve these disputes, and here are some suggestions of what should be the benchmarks," says Zack.[32] He solicited input from a wide variety of labor and management organizations, incorporating their feedback and that of commission task force members into a single document that was then put to a vote. "[T]he achievement of agreement on the components of the document did mark a substantial step forward in providing due process protections in procedures where many such protections had been lacking," concludes Zack.[33]

In his 1996 presentation, Dunlop was decidedly hopeful about the prospects for expanding the use of private mediation and arbitration in employment law disputes. His scholarly taunting of Zack had resulted in a protocol with the potential to be adopted by a wide range of employers. In the year after the commission wrapped up its work, a number of states and government agencies adopted programs of voluntary arbitration. The Massachusetts Commission Against Discrimination began settling cases via voluntary arbitration and mediation, while the federal Equal Employment Opportunity Council began utilizing mediation in order to resolve its extensive backlog of cases. The NLRB, meanwhile, had begun an experiment with "settlement judges" as an alternative to lengthy and expensive court cases. And President Clinton had thrown his support behind alternative dispute resolution, issuing an executive order intended to further its use in civil justice reform, and signing into law the Administrative Resolution Act of 1996, authorizing and supporting both negotiated rule-making and alternative dispute resolution as a method of adjudicating disputes.[34]

In his 2002 interview, Dunlop recounted the failure of the Clinton commission's legislative proposals with blunt matter-of-factness. He'd never expected that the commission's whole set of proposals would simply appear on the Hill, Dunlop told interviewer Bruce Kaufman. "That's not how things work there, and I have been around long enough to know this."[35] But as he noted, the change in the political climate had made even piecemeal adoption of the recommendations impractical. And so he had moved on, Dunlop explained focusing his time and attention on the areas where he saw the most potential to make changes. "It's a long-run process and change happens only slowly," said Dunlop, "but I remain optimistic."[36]

NOTES

1. Dunlop made the statement to his colleagues David Weil and Fred Abernathy. Recounted by Weil in an interview with the author, September 11, 2017.
2. Bruce E. Kaufman. "Reflections on Six Decades in Industrial Relations: An Interview with John Dunlop." *Industrial and Labor Relations Review*, 55, no. 2 (January 2002): 347.
3. In 1993, Dunlop was two years into the massive textile research project that would eventually culminate in a book, a *Stitch in Time*, written with collaborators David Weil, Fred Abernathy and Jan Hammond. Weil, who was then in his early 30's, remembers wondering where he would find the energy to manage all the research the group was undertaking and his other activities as a professor. "And here was John, at 80," recalls Weil.
4. Quinn Mills, interviewed by the author, June 21, 2016.
5. Kaufman, p. 342.
6. John T. Dunlop, "The Commission and Alternative Dispute Resolution," Paper presented at the Society of Professionals in Dispute Resolution conference, October 24, 1996, Anaheim, CA.
7. Ibid.
8. Frank Swoboda, "Labor Commission's Head Looks at Unshackling Cooperation on the Job," *Washington Post*, July 4, 1993.
9. Thomas A. Kochan, *Shaping the Future of Work*, (New York: Business Expert Press, 2016),115.
10. Fact Finding Report: Dunlop Commission on the Future of Worker-Management Relations, May 1994, xii.
11. Kaufman, p. 342.
12. Louis Uchitelle, "A Call for Easing Labor-Management Tension," *New York Times*, May 30, 1994.
13. Ibid.
14. The Dunlop Commission on the Future of Worker-Management Relations, Final Report, December 1, 1994, 8.
15. Weil interview.
16. John T. Dunlop and Richard D. Bartel, "Working Towards Consensus," *Challenge*, 25, no. 3 (1982), pp. 32–33.
17. Weil interview.
18. Dunlop Commission, Final Report, Dissenting Opinion of Douglas A. Fraser, in Section 2, p. 12.
19. Tom Donahue, interviewed by the author, March 23, 2016.
20. Ibid.
21. Ibid.
22. Kaufman, p. 344.
23. Ibid.
24. Tom Kochan, interviewed by the author, May 3, 2016.
25. Ibid.
26. Ibid.
27. Dunlop "The Commission and Alternative Dispute Resolution."
28. Ibid., 4.
29. Arnold Zack, "The Due Process Protocol: Getting There and Getting Over It," *Employee Rights and Employment Policy Journal*, 11, no. 2 (2007): 102..
30. See Chapter IV of the Fact Finding Report, Section IV, 30–33.
31. Zack, p. 102.
32. Arnold Zack, interviewed by the author, April 4, 2016.
33. Zack, p, 104.
34. Dunlop, 1996, 7–8.
35. Kaufman, p. 343.
36. Ibid., p. 345.

Chapter Seven

Cucumbers and Tomatoes

Yo soy Juan Dunlop.

This was how Dunlop introduced himself to the farmworkers who toiled in fields of Northwest Ohio. It was late in the summer of 1985 and Dunlop had made the trek to the Midwest in an effort to resolve what would turn out to be one of the most challenging disputes of his career. What he referred to as the "cucumbers and tomatoes" was a complex, multi-faceted problem involving agricultural workers, mostly undocumented, who had no protections to speak of under US labor law, the growers who relied on their seasonal labor, and giant food processing corporations, including Campbell Soup, which purchased the crops, but claimed no responsibility for the pay of the farmworkers or their working conditions. Crafting a lasting solution would require not just bringing the assorted parties to the table after years of rancor and high-profile protests but creating a "tripartite" mechanism for solving future problems.

Dunlop's success in confronting the problem can be measured in the Dunlop Commission's continued existence—and evolution—more than three decades later. And unlike much of his non-academic work, an unusual record of Dunlop's thought processes around his problem-solving techniques exists in the form of a video recording of a class he conducted at the Harvard Business School in 1990.[1] This rare document sheds light, not just on how Dunlop went about mediating a resolution to the bitter battle between the farmworkers, their union and the food companies, but offers intriguing insights into his approach to problem solving more generally.

SEARCHING FOR A SOLUTION

The phone rang in Ray Goldberg's office at the Harvard Business School one morning in the winter of 1985. At the other end was Gordon McGovern, the president and CEO of Campbell Soup. McGovern needed some advice. The campaign against Campbell by the farmworkers who picked tomatoes and cucumbers for the company's products had dragged on for nearly a decade—and seemed to be picking up steam. Did Goldberg happen to know an expert in labor relations at Harvard named John Dunlop?[2]

That McGovern chose to call Goldberg for assistance wasn't entirely surprising. The two had been classmates at the business school in 1950, and Goldberg, who was not just the founder of the agribusiness program at Harvard, but had coined the very term "agribusiness," had deep food industry ties. The head of the Private and Public, Scientific, Academic, and Consumer Food Policy Group, or PAPSAC, Goldberg regularly brought together representatives of the US food industry, including labor unions, to talk about the rapid transformation of the nation's agricultural sector. He had also given a number of presentations on the future of the food system to the Grocery Manufacturers annual meeting at McGovern's request. McGovern's invitation to the event, held at notoriously remote golf course, even included transportation. "He was kind enough to let me hitch a ride on the company plane," recalls Goldberg.[3]

And yet on this day, McGovern had reached Goldberg almost by accident. He'd made his first call to the Harvard switchboard, only then recalling that he had a connection on the faculty. Still, it would have been hard for the Campbell CEO to find anyone who was as knowledgeable about Dunlop and his approach to labor/management problem solving as Ray Goldberg. Their relationship dated back more than four decades, to when Goldberg, then an undergraduate from Fargo, North Dakota, had signed up for Dunlop's course in labor relations.

"Dunlop taught the course by assigning one person to be labor, one person to be management and one person to play the part of John Dunlop," recalls Goldberg. "I was mesmerized by how he was able to convince people who normally thought of themselves as enemies to think of themselves as partners."[4] Goldberg was eager to learn more and invited Dunlop to sit down for an interview at the Harvard radio station for a far-reaching exchange in which Dunlop talked about his background as the son of a missionary, his work in labor relations both on and off campus, and his views on the tenuous nature of democracy. "I really saw him as a changemaker with respect to labor, private and public life," says Goldberg.[5]

Goldberg and Dunlop would go on to become close colleagues at the Harvard Business School, a professional relationship that lasted until Dunlop's death. As Goldberg notes, he and Dunlop shared a passion for understanding the role that the food sector played in the larger economy. When Dunlop authored *Lessons of Wage and Price Controls: The Food Sector* in 1979, detailing the dramatic run-up in food prices during the '70's and the largely futile efforts to control costs, it was Goldberg whom he asked to write the section on agriculture. And when Dunlop led a major study on the impact of mechanization upon US garment manufacturers, Goldberg facilitated a partnership with cotton industry leaders.

On that morning in 1984, though, Goldberg presented to the Campbell CEO a greatly abbreviated version of his connection to John Dunlop. He brought McGovern up to speed on Dunlop's background and his approach to problem solving, offering to do his part to bring the two men together. McGovern eagerly accepted his offer, and while it would be months before he and Dunlop would meet in person, the wheels had been set in motion for what would become one of the most meaningful challenges of Dunlop's long career.

By the time McGovern went in search of Dunlop, the strife between Campbell Soup and migrant tomato and cucumber pickers in the Midwest had been simmering for nearly a decade; efforts to improve the workers' lot through unionization dated back even further. The Farm Worker Organizing Committee (FLOC) had been formed in 1968 to organize migrant farm workers, primarily Mexican Americans, who made the annual trek from Texas or Florida to work in the fields of Northwest Ohio and Southern Michigan.[6] Under the leadership of Baldemar Velásquez, the son of migrant farmworkers and then a college student in Ohio, FLOC sought to organize farmworkers on a farm-by-farm basis. While a three-day strike by tomato pickers resulted in contracts with 21 growers, the real battle was only beginning, recalls Velásquez. "The following year they tried to displace the union members with new workers."[7] The union filed suit—and won—but Velásquez and other FLOC leaders were increasingly convinced that they needed another strategy besides organizing workers farm-by-farm.

A major part of the problem lay with the structure of the market for tomatoes and other specialty crops. The growers had little ability to boost wages or offer better benefits unless they secured more lucrative terms from the food processors that purchased their crops. And because farmers who grew the kinds of specialty crops that the migrant pickers in the Midwest were harvesting typically contracted with a single company to purchase the entire season's production, they had little bargaining power. Growers who tried to charge more for their produce quickly found themselves out of business thanks to the highly competitive nature of the market. FLOC had been focusing all of its efforts at the bottom of the supply chain, but the real power was concentrated at the top, with the food-processors and manufacturers. Another season of difficult negotiations with individual growers in Ohio convinced FLOC's leaders that the time for a different approach had arrived.

Explains Velásquez: “If the manufacturers did not put more money into the bottom of their supply chain, we would never get the wages and benefits that workers deserved.”[8]

In 1970, FLOC pivoted towards what the organizers described as a “supply chain strategy,” targeting the largest single purchaser of tomatoes in Northwestern Ohio: the Campbell Soup Company, or as it was familiarly known, Campbell’s. The ultimate goal, says Velásquez, was to pressure the food processing giant to engage in a three-way negotiation with growers and the union, something that had never been done before.[9] And that required forcing Campbell to acknowledge having *any* direct responsibility for the seasonal workers who picked the crops that the company bought. FLOC began laying the groundwork for a broader campaign, one focused on building a broad social alliance behind its demands and making the pubic case that corporations like Campbell owed something to the farmworkers.

FLOC issued an official call for three-way negotiations in the spring of 1978, inviting growers and corporations to meet with the union to discuss the working conditions in the fields. Only a few growers responded, while the corporations ignored FLOC’s summons completely. It was time to raise the stakes. That summer, during the height of tomato season, some 2,000 FLOC supporters in Ohio went on strike, refusing to pick the crop and picketing area tomato processing plants. But again, FLOC proved unable to force Campbell Soup to negotiate directly with the union. Campbell responded to the strike by reiterating that it had no relationship with the Midwestern farm workers, then mandating that its growers mechanize their harvests in hopes of skirting the farm labor issue entirely.[10]

When Congress enacted the National Labor Relations Act in 1935 to protect the rights of employees and encourage collective bargaining, farm workers, and domestic workers, were excluded from its protections. Historians continue to debate the reason for this—whether it reflected the rural composition of the legislature, the influence of Southern racism or the dominance at that time of the agricultural sector by small family farms. For Velásquez and his FLOC organizers, the absence of labor protections for farm workers meant that, while the workers could still form unions, the farmers were under no statutory obligation to recognize them. “We had to be creative because we didn’t have a labor law,” says Velásquez.[11]

As Velásquez saw it, FLOC had no choice but to make its campaign to raise the wages of migrant farm workers and improve their working conditions a social justice crusade. “Our goal was to put enough pressure on Campbell Soup so that they would have to do something to make us go away,” says Velásquez.[12] If FLOC succeeded in forcing Campbell to negotiate, the union could use a similar approach with other companies. With limited resources and an ambitious agenda, FLOC launched a nationwide consumer boycott of Campbell in 1979. The boycott would last for six years, attracting broad popular support among students, labor unions, immigrant rights organizations and church groups, including influential leaders within the Catholic church. Unions donated funds and encouraged their members to join in the boycott. Religious organizations did the same, with Catholic, Jewish, mainstream Protestant as well as interfaith groups signing onto the boycott. In their history of FLOC, Barger and Reza argue that the farmworkers' cause caught on because it appealed to basic American values of social justice and human dignity. They estimate that more than 1 million Americans took part in the boycott.[13]

The summer of 1983 marked a turning point. For four long years, FLOC leaders and farm workers had been traveling the country, speaking to anyone who would listen about the boycott and the working conditions of the migrant tomato pickers. That summer, 100 farm workers marched more than 600 miles, from FLOC's headquarters in Toledo, Ohio to Camden, NJ, the site of Campbell's corporate offices. The marchers were greeted in Philadelphia and Camden by massive rallies and, for the first time, national media attention.

Campbell was paying attention too. In 1980, the company offered the Ohio Council of Churches $250,000 for services for migrant workers but was rebuffed by the group. And in 1982, representatives from FLOC and Campbell met in Cambridge, MA for exploratory discussions—a sign of the company's growing concerns over the union's tactics. The talks went nowhere, however, and FLOC's campaign continued to expand. When Jesse Jackson mentioned the boycott in his nationally televised speech at the Democratic convention in the summer of 1984, it was a sign of just how far the farm workers and their cause had traveled. FLOC's demand for a signed contract with Campbell was now coming from an astonishing array of voices.

When Campbell CEO Gordon McGovern went in search of John Dunlop, it was just as Velásquez had hoped: the company was desperate to make FLOC go away. But what would that mean?

AN INTRIGUING CASE

The first person Dunlop would speak to about Campbell's labor troubles wasn't McGovern himself, but his emissary Ray Page, a company vice president. "His first question for me was 'how much do you charge?'" Dunlop recounted in the 1990 video of his talk to Ray Goldberg's students at the Harvard Business School.[14] Dunlop, who was by then an emeritus faculty member, was as blunt with the students as he had been with Page. Taking money from Campbell would compromise his ability to hammer out a solution that both sides could live with. "I'm not a consultant," Dunlop told the students.[15]

Even by Dunlop's standards, the decade-long dispute between the farm workers and Campbell Soup presented an unusually complex set of problems. In the recording of his visit to Ray Goldberg's class, Dunlop gave the students a glimpse into the thinking behind his approach. "He tried to explain to the students how you find a methodology that enables people who have differences to find common ground," recalls Goldberg.[16]

To begin with, there was the challenge of untangling the various parties that were involved in the dispute. There was FLOC and the 7,000 migrant farm workers who made the trek to pick tomatoes and cucumbers in the fields of Michigan and Ohio each year. There were the family farmers who provided crops to Campbell and its subsidiaries. There was also Campbell itself, which had succeeded in largely mechanizing the tomato harvest during the years of the FLOC dispute but still required millions of tons of hand-picked cucumbers for its Vlasic pickle brand. There was also the tomato processing plant in Northwestern, Ohio, whose employees were represented by another union, the United Food and Commercial Workers, which was strongly opposed to FLOC. And these were only the parties that were, more or less, directly involved in the controversy. FLOC's ten-year long crusade had succeeded in building a coalition that extended far beyond those direct parties. Church groups in Ohio and beyond had played a key role in the boycott from its inception. Should they also be part of the effort to reach a solution?

In the classroom with Goldberg's students, who'd been reading a teaching case on migrant farmworkers in the Midwest, Dunlop chalked out a diagram on the blackboard, lines and squiggles indicating the assorted actors. Swirls and arrows indicated where there was a relationship between the various parties. The diagram, rough as it was, served to make his larger point: that each of the individual parts of the complex equation existed in relationship to the others. Touch one and you affect the totality. "I hope sooner or later that you learn that all of us who make decisions have to deal with the totality of life," Dunlop told the students, growing serious and philosophical. "You do not make decisions on part of it."[17]

Then there was the question of who spoke for the various parties—or who were the 'principals,' in Dunlopian parlance—and whether they had the backing and the seriousness of purpose that would be necessary to carry off the kind of negotiations that Dunlop had in mind. While his initial conversation with Ray Page had been fruitful, Dunlop couldn't yet determine the extent to which Page spoke for Campbell. He insisted on meeting with Gordon McGovern directly, to discern, among other things, how serious Campbell was about crafting a long-term solution to its labor problems in the Midwest. Dunlop also needed to know much more about FLOC organizer Baldemar Velásquez. It was clear that he was able to deliver fiery speeches and lead marches, Dunlop told the students, "but does he have the potential to be a business unionist?"[18]

For information about Velásquez, Dunlop turned to 'labor priest' Monsignor George Higgins, who'd been a strong supporter of the Campbell boycott. Then, in the spring of 1985, Dunlop and Velásquez finally met face to face. The meeting, which Dunlop had arranged to take place at the Harvard Club in New York City, did not get off to an auspicious beginning. Velásquez, unaware of the club's strict dress code, had shown up without a tie, and the two had been shown the door. "He got in a huff and a puff," recalls Velásquez.[19] Fortunately they were able to find some less august spot nearby, and their hours long conversation could begin at last.

If Dunlop had questions about Velásquez, the FLOC organizer had plenty that he wanted to impress upon 'the professor,' as he would come to refer to him. While Velásquez was encouraged that Campbell had felt enough pressure to bring in a labor relations specialist, he was concerned that the company was looking for a prominent figure to give credibility to a cosmetic solution: a blue ribbon-style commission that would recommend a social service approach rather than the union contract that FLOC sought. When Dunlop asked him to tell him about the issue with Campbell, Velásquez did just that.

As the afternoon wore on, Velásquez systematically laid out what FLOC had been campaigning for, and how the union had arrived at the conclusion that direct negotiations with Campbell were the only solution. He broke down for Dunlop the various elements of the production chain: a simple three-party chain in the case of tomatoes; a more complex four or even five-party-chain with cucumbers. "I've looked at this. I've studied it. I've crunched numbers with the farmers," Velásquez explained.[20] He pulled out a piece of paper and did the math. If the average yield per acre was 16 tons and the growers were getting just $34 per ton, there was no way the farmers could pay the laborers more. "It makes no sense to negotiate with the growers. Campbell controls every aspect of the supply chain," said Velásquez.[21]

Dunlop took it all in, interrupting with questions and jotting down occasional notes. "Under what conditions would you be willing to call off the boycott?" he asked finally. Velásquez didn't even have to consider the question. "When we have a signed agreement with Campbell and the growers, recognizing FLOC." The response, recalls Velásquez, came with a 'jowly grin'—a look he would come to know as a signature Dunlop expression. "Fair enough," said Dunlop.[22]

INTO THE FIELDS

While it had taken FLOC almost a decade to get Campbell to respond to the farmworker's demands, the process of trying to solve the dispute suddenly sped into high gear. Within weeks of his conversation with Dunlop, Velásquez was in Toledo meeting with Campbell VP, Ray Page. Over the course of six hours, they hammered out a memorandum of understanding, laying out the details for the three-way labor agreement that would come to be known as the Dunlop Commission.

FLOC nominated four representatives, as did the growers. Dunlop, who served as chairman, selected two nominees from each side, a mix of labor and business leaders that included former UAW President Douglas Fraser; Thomas Anderson, the chief of an Ohio grain company; Monsignor George Higgins; along with an agricultural economist from Purdue University, Don Paarlberg.

Missing from the list were the direct parties to the conflict: FLOC and Campbell. As Dunlop explained to the students in Goldberg's class, he had handpicked individuals who could apply pressure to both sides if necessary. It would be up to Anderson to keep Campbell in line, while both of the labor representatives could do the same with the FLOC head, especially Monsignor Higgins, "who [Velásquez] has respect for in this world and the next," said Dunlop.[23]

The Dunlop Commission's very first task would also be among its most important: holding elections to determine whether the workers in Ohio and Michigan wanted to be represented by FLOC. In August of 1985, Dunlop made the trek to the Midwest along with Glenn Fine, a lawyer from the AFL-CIO, and Alida Castillo, a young research assistant from Harvard who'd agreed to serve as Dunlop's translator.[24] And in a sign of the collaborative spirit of the enterprise—something that would have been almost impossible to imagine just a few months before—the delegation was joined by representatives from FLOC, Campbell, and its subsidiary, Vlasic.[25]

"It wasn't an antagonistic thing," recalls Castillo. "The representatives from the companies really seemed like they wanted to make this work. They wanted us to help them resolve this situation."[26]

Over the course of a week, the group would visit some 20 farms in both states, handing out union cards and explaining to the workers that they had the right to vote—a novel concept for a group that had rarely, if ever, been asked to vote on anything. The troupe of visitors, a seventy-year-old professor at its center, was likely somewhat startling for the farm workers; Castillo recalls that many of the workers on the farms would simply scattered out of fear that the visitors were from immigration. Others were curious about the gentleman at the group's center, who seemed to be able to tell the farmers to "do this and do that."[27]

As for Dunlop himself, he seemed to relish the opportunity to talk directly with the workers whose working and living conditions had been the object of inquiry and investigation for months now. These visits with the farm workers and their families were the highlight of the trip, says Castillo. "John would sit there with the migrant workers, just chatting with them and their wives, hearing about what their lives were like," recalls Castillo. At night, Dunlop would regale their group with stories about all of the important people he'd met throughout his career. But with the workers, he brought a more modest and humble front, says Castillo. "He was very respectful and empathetic with them."[28]

As they made their way from farm to farm, Dunlop and his crew also got to see close up the transformation of agricultural production. Where the tomato harvest had been mechanized, the fruit, green and solid, was scooped off the vine by machine, then moved along a conveyor belt. The new process required a fraction of the labor that a hand-picked crop like cucumbers necessitated. But for the workers who tended the fast-moving belt, it was still grueling, and the pace of the conveyor was a matter over which FLOC wanted to negotiate.

Meanwhile, union elections were held on each of the farms according to a prearranged schedule. In contrast to the early days of FLOC organizing, when violent altercations between farmers and organizers were all too common, all was peaceful this time around. As part of the lead up to the elections, the union, the growers and Campbell had all agreed to try to keep the process free of unfair labor practices. "It worked remarkably well," says Velásquez. "Some of the growers were trying to get their family members to vote but it wasn't enough to affect the outcome."[29]

The cards were packed up and returned to Cambridge, where they would be counted by a young Harvard economist named Richard Freeman, a former student of Dunlop's. Freeman's job was to assess whether votes had been cast by workers or management, a task he carried out at his kitchen table. Some of these judgment calls were obvious, recalls Freeman. The crew chief was clearly management. But what about his wife and children, who were part of the crew? "It wasn't the easiest task," says Freeman.[30]

That there was no formal agency involved in overseeing this process is a testament to the amount of trust that both FLOC and Campbell had so quickly placed in Dunlop. It was also typical of the way that Dunlop approached his problem-solving work, says Freeman. "He preferred operating person-to-person. He could get people to come and do things informally, trusting that everyone wanted a resolution."[31]

A THREE-WAY CONTRACT

When the votes were finally tallied, farm workers on three quarters of the farms where elections were held had chosen FLOC to be their representative. The vote cleared the way for a series of discussions between union representatives, Campbell, tomato growers, and members of the newly-formed Dunlop Commission. Held between October and November 1985, the exchanges were wide ranging, venturing beyond the specific problems of the growers and their migrant workers to address the larger economic context of the tomato industry. These initial conversations laid the groundwork for more formal contract deliberations. The pace was quick, in part because the National Council of Churches continued to hold out the threat of endorsing the FLOC boycott if a contract wasn't reached by February 21, 1986.[32]

The parties would meet that deadline, and on February 23, went public with the news that nearly a decade of strife between Campbell Soup and the migrant laborers who picked its tomatoes was over at last.[33] FLOC's first contract was a novel three-way agreement that included the union, Campbell Soup, and a newly created organization of vegetable growers known as the Campbell Growers Association. It was the first such three-way labor agreement between workers, their employer and their employer's major customer in the country, as well as the first farm labor contract in the US outside of California. Most importantly, Campbell was agreeing to foot the cost for raising farm worker wages and improving their working conditions.

The agreement, which was signed in Detroit, home to Dunlop Commission member and former UAW chief Doug Fraser, included much of what FLOC had been fighting for. The workers had won a significant pay increase and a new grievance procedure, along with the promise of better housing, health and safety protections and the eventual end to a sharecropping system that classified farm workers as independent contractors. Migrant workers who traveled to the same farms season after season would get preferential hiring for future seasons. The growers, meanwhile, received a guarantee from Campbell that the processing giant would purchase a fixed portion of their crops each year, while the company was assured a steady supply of produce.

And while it was tensions over tomatoes that had thrust the farm workers into the spotlight, the most important provisions of the contract had to do with cucumbers. Even as Dunlop worked to resolve the disputes between Campbell and FLOC and set up a forum for future problem solving, it was increasingly obvious that the mechanization of the tomato crop was essentially eliminating the need for farm labor. The agreement also included provisions that would allow FLOC a foothold in the cucumber industry. Some 70 cucumber farms, all under contract to Campbell or one of its subsidiaries, had agreed to let their workers vote on whether they wanted FLOC to represent them. If 50 percent of workers on the new farms signaled their assent by signing cards they would be brought under the just-signed contract, while the cucumber growers would become part of a growers' association and part of the larger Dunlop Commission structure.

Within a few short years, FLOC would unionize the entire cucumber industry in Northwest Ohio, bringing growers and major food processors, including Vlasic and Dean Foods, under the terms of the initial agreement. Velásquez attributes the vision behind the union's success to Cesar Chavez, founder of the United Farm Workers. "He's the one who taught me that when you have a first contract, and you have the company on the ropes, you better ask for anything you can get."[34] But the mechanics of realizing that vision were entirely the work of John Dunlop, says Velásquez. It was Dunlop's idea, for example, to include language in the contract specifying that workers could organize via card check. It was his idea again that growers and processors would agree to become part of the commission as a condition of a settlement. "He had a real sense of the big picture and the future of the industry, but the real brilliance of John Dunlop was that he understood how to make things happen."[35]

NEW PROBLEMS, NEW POSSIBILITIES

By the time Dunlop accepted Goldberg's invitation to speak to his class at the Harvard Business School in September of 1990, the Dunlop Commission's experiment with three-way negotiations in Ohio and Michigan was four years old. By Dunlop's own measure, the effort had been a success. He had set out in 1985, not just to help negotiate an end to FLOC's boycott of Campbell Soup, but to establish an ongoing institutional forum for all of the major parties involved in the dispute.

While Dean Foods wouldn't become signatory to the agreement until 1991, Heinz was now a participant. Bringing new companies under the commission umbrella was essential, as otherwise those businesses that agreed to foot the cost of providing better conditions for farm workers could end up losing out to competitors with lower costs. And so far, the commission had managed to carefully navigate this tricky terrain without running afoul of antitrust laws.[36] The body was even making progress in having the migrant cucumber workers reclassified as employees, another delicate negotiation as the Fair Labor Standards Act required that each individual employee earn the minimum wage, a regulation that didn't easily apply to migrants who often worked as families and were paid by the bushel.

Dunlop concluded his discussion with Goldberg's students by taking stock of what the commission had accomplished so far, making clear that there remained plenty of problems still to be solved. "The work is never done," he told the students. "There are always new problems and new possibilities."[37]

More than three decades after Dunlop helped to establish the first three-way labor agreement in the country and a unique forum for addressing problems in the agricultural industry, the Dunlop Commission remains very much alive. In 2004, its reach was extended to North Carolina, where commission members brokered another three-way contract, this one between FLOC, the Mt. Olive Pickle company, and a new growers association. Like the original Campbell deal, this one was also precedent setting. It was the first labor agreement in US history to involve guest workers, who traveled from Mexico to North Carolina each summer as part of the H-2A visa program.[38] Because the workers were considered independent contractors, they weren't covered by the Fair Labor Standards Act (FLSA) or by the Migrant and Seasonal Agricultural Worker Protection Act (MSPA). Winning protections for the workers required first changing their status, something Dunlop was able to pull off only by personally intervening on their behalf at both the Department of Labor and the Internal Revenue Service.

"It was really pretty remarkable, when you think about it," says David Weil, who would help to lead the commission after Dunlop's death. "In a state with the lowest union density, in a sector with the lowest union density, you now had a contract that covered guest workers."[39] Weil, who went on to oversee the Wage and Hour Division of the Department of Labor under the Obama Administration from 2014 to the beginning of 2017, is convinced that the model created by Dunlop to address the crisis of farm labor remains powerful for agriculture, and has potential for other sectors with lots of workers who aren't covered by traditional labor law, including domestic workers, home care workers, and the growing number of independent contractors who lack a traditional employer. The challenge, says Weil, is to approach the task of winning protections for such workers the way that Dunlop did. "Some people might have looked at agricultural workers and said, 'well, they're not covered by the NLRA so there's nothing we can do. Or they'd conclude that we have to pass a law. But John was never bound by that kind of thinking," says Weil.[40]

NOTES

1. Video recording of Ray Goldberg class, September 26, 1990.
2. Ray Goldberg, interviewed by the author, June 16, 2016.
3. Ibid.
4. Ibid.
5. Ibid.
6. Michael Kennedy, "Migrant Farmworkers in the Midwest," case study, (Boston: Harvard Business Publishing, 1985.)
7. Baldemar Velásquez, email correspondence with the author, June 30, 2017.

8. Baldemar Velásquez, interviewed by the author, July 20, 2016.
9. Ibid.
10. W.K. Barger and Ernesto Reza, *The Farm Labor Movement in the Midwest*, (Austin, TX: University of Texas Press, 1994) 64.
11. Baldemar Velásquez, interviewed by the author, September 24, 2014.
12. Ibid.
13. Barger and Reza, p. 67.
14. Video of Goldberg's class, 1990.
15. Ibid.
16. Golderg interview.
17. Video of Goldberg's class.
18. Ibid.
19. Velásquez interview.
20. Ibid.
21. Ibid.
22. Ibid.
23. Ibid.
24. Alida Castillo, interviewed by the author, July 26, 2016.
25. The trip, as well as subsequent commission expenses, were paid for through a grant from the Carnegie Endowment in New York. While Campbell Soup had earlier indicated a willingness to fund the work of the commission, Dunlop rejected this idea in favor of a more neutral funding source. Cited in Kennedy, 1985.
26. Castillo interview.
27. Ibid.
28. Ibid.
29. Velásquez interview.
30. Interview with Richard Freeman, July 20, 2016.
31. Ibid.
32. Kennedy, 1985, 4.
33. Keith Schneider, "Campbell Soup Accord Ends Decade of Strife," *New York Times*, February 23, 1986.
34. Velásquez interview.
35. Ibid.
36. Because higher prices often result when competitors agree to restrict competition, the Dunlop Commission had to be very careful that its three-way agreements didn't cross the line into price fixing.
37. Video of Goldberg's class.
38. Teófilo Reyes, "8000 'Guest Workers' Join Farm Union in North Carolina," *Labor Notes*, September 30, 2004.
39. David Weil, remarks to the "Farm Labor Challenges" conference, Harvard University, November 12, 2014.
40. David Weil, interviewed by the author, May 4, 2016.

Chapter Eight

A Stitch in Time

In his memoir of the 1969 Harvard wars, Roger Rosenblatt describes crossing Harvard Yard with John Dunlop, and, in an effort to engage him in conversation, mentioning a news item about a manned flight to Mars. Dunlop, recounts the writer, smiled, his response exultant: "More worlds to negotiate!"[1] While Dunlop's passion for solving problems and mediating disputes wouldn't take him as far as Mars, his work spanned an enormous array of 'worlds.' "The range of his interests was extraordinary," wrote George Shultz after the death of his long-time friend and colleague. "But this range was not the mark of a dilettante. Somehow he found the time to dig in deeply at whatever he undertook."[2]

Even in this vast constellation of interests, Dunlop's seven-year-long adventure in the apparel industry, aimed at both understanding it from top to bottom and helping it recover from the ravages of global competition, stands out. The project began in 1991 as an academic undertaking, after Dunlop and his long-time Harvard colleague Fred Abernathy, a professor of mechanical engineering, received a grant from the Alfred P. Sloan Foundation to study the textile and apparel industries. While the two had done work together in this field a decade before, the $2 million Sloan grant, part of the foundation's Industry Studies program aimed at helping embattled American industries recover, would enable them to focus on the subject in earnest. The primary vehicle for their systematic exploration into the transformation of the two industries was the newly created Harvard Center for Textile and Apparel Research, or HCTAR, led by four "investigators": Abernathy, Dunlop, Janice Hammond, a professor at the Harvard Business School, and David Weil, a young economics professor at Boston University and a former PhD student of Dunlop's.

Their investigations would lead to a book, *Stitch in Time*, and take the researchers all over the world as they sought to understand how technological change and the rise of "lean retailing" was remaking an entire industry. A fifth colleague, computer scientist Victor Milenkovic, worked on a corollary project, applying the ideas and techniques of computation geometry to make the layout of apparel parts more efficient. In all, the enterprise would last for more than eight years, a few years longer than what Dunlop considered the minimum required for a serious study. "John would always say 'a problem isn't worth studying if you're not going to stay with it for five years,'" recalls Weil. "You're not going to learn the players, the dynamics, the data."[3]

The first phase of what the investigators referred to as HCTAR, for their Harvard center, kicked off with a gathering of the major industry players for a convening that came to be known as the Shirt Workshop. Top executives, retailers, apparel and textile producers, representatives from relevant government agencies, along with the heads of both apparel unions were summoned to Harvard to discuss the problems confronting the American shirt industry. The event bore several hallmarks of a classically Dunlopian approach, says Weil. It came together quickly, relied heavily upon Dunlop's famous rolodex, and most importantly, the two-day convening produced genuine insights: a new way to think about what was happening in the apparel and textile industries. "What was really amazing was that we came out with this systems analysis. It wasn't about making shirts. It was about the fact that the retail sector had changed," says Weil.[4] What the investigators were beginning to comprehend was that the industry itself was undergoing a fundamental transformation, moving from a world in which inventory was built up over time, based largely on guesswork regarding what would sell, to one in which demand was driven by data in real time.

HCTAR also shared another classic element of Dunlop's favored way of doing business: an intense collaboration with colleagues whom he liked and admired. His connection to Abernathy, known to Dunlop as "Freddy," went back to the late 60's and the Harvard wars. Their paths crossed again while Abernathy was in Washington, working as the Director of Engineering for the National Science Foundation and Dunlop was overseeing the Cost of Living Council. As Abernathy recalls, if he wanted to get an audience with Dunlop to discuss what was happening at Harvard, he had to follow the same protocol as everyone else. "He'd say 'meet me in the Old Rogue's Bar at the Statler Hotel across from the White House.' He'd be in a booth at the back and you'd have various union people from the building trades come up and talk about why Bill or Tom or Dick hated John in Los Angeles. Dunlop said it was my education," says Abernathy.[5] And when Abernathy was back in Washington, this time to run the NSF, it was his old friend Dunlop who talked him into returning to Harvard. "[If you come back to Harvard you can do anything you want. Down here in Washington you always work for somebody else."[6]

TC²

Abernathy did indeed return to Harvard, and soon after, he and Dunlop teamed up on a project to introduce robotics to the sewing of men's suits, known as TC², or the Tailored Clothing Technology Corporation.[7] The leader of the Amalgamated Clothing and Textile Workers, Murray Finley, foresaw that the migration of jobs in his industry to lower wage countries meant doom for American textile workers and enlisted Dunlop to study the extent of the problem. While the data looked bleak indeed, Dunlop suggested a possible path to survival: a joint labor/management training program, funded by the government, and aimed at boosting employee retention and productivity, as well as an effort to improve quality in the industry. The joint training initiative was quickly rolled out under the Department of Labor's Comprehensive Employment and Training Act (CETA) program and was, according to Dunlop's own assessment, "well organized and efficiently managed."[8] While the training program wouldn't survive the arrival of President Reagan, another of Dunlop's recommendations, a research and development program, would prove much longer lived.

The R and D effort focused on a key and seemingly counterintuitive question: could more textile jobs be saved if parts of the production process were roboticized? To help answer that question, Dunlop enlisted the help of the engineer he knew best: Fred Abernathy. As Dunlop recounted in his 1984 volume, *Dispute Resolution: Negotiation and Consensus Building*, Abernathy's role was to explore opportunities for genuine R and D in an industry that had no history of it. And by encouraging technological development, Dunlop's hope was that a sector made up overwhelmingly of women and minorities could avoid a rapid dislocation of workers. "The parties, it might be said, are seeking modestly to develop an element of their own industrial policy appropriate to the sector," noted Dunlop. [9]

Dunlop and Abernathy presented their findings at a workshop in August of 1979, which in turn led to the establishment of a non-profit corporation, TC², the following year. The board of directors of the new organization included representatives of clothing and textile companies, cloth and synthetic fiber manufacturers and other interested parties. The project's funding reflected its tripartite nature, with the union and each company chipping in $50,000 and the remainder provided through Department of Commerce funds designated for trade-afflicted industries.[10]

By the end of its first year, TC² even had a prototype machine, designed by MIT's Draper Labs. In 1983, the machine, which used computer-designed cloth cutting technologies to sew men's sleeves, was being tested at a production facility in Allentown, PA. The researchers would ultimately conclude that robotics did not represent a cost-effective replacement for skilled sewers. But the collaboration between Abernathy and Dunlop endured. Dunlop called upon his friend's knowledge of things regularly during their work together in the textile and apparel industries, as well as a later effort to make homebuilding in the US more efficient.

Dunlop's relationship with David Weil was more recent. Weil had encountered Dunlop as a master's student while taking a class with labor economist and Dunlop protégé Jim Medoff. While Weil knew of Dunlop by reputation he says that he mostly avoided him because "he was so fricking scary."[11] But the lure of what Dunlop did proved irresistible, and Weil would become one of his last PhD students, forging a bond that lasted until Dunlop died. The HCTAR project represented the first time that Weil and Dunlop would work together as colleagues. "John reached out to me and said 'would you like to work on a grant with me?'" Weil, who had recently begun teaching economics at the Boston University School of Management, said he thought about it for 'half a second.' "I said I would love to."[12]

With the aid of Janice Hammond, a young professor at the Harvard Business School, the team of investigators would begin a top to bottom examination of the retail and apparel industries, as viewed through the systemic lens that had emerged from the initial Harvard gathering. The collaborative spirit reflected in that first meeting would infuse the project at every step of the way. As they collected information—from site visits, case studies and survey data gleaned from more than sixty pages of questions completed by 118 business units—the group constantly tested and refined their ideas and results by consulting with business leaders, union representatives and government officials.[13] An advisory committee of such experts, a hallmark of so many of Dunlop's undertakings, was set up to provide guidance. Meanwhile, monthly seminars at Harvard provided a forum for the team to test its ideas while serving the essential function of "reigning in intellectual exuberance."[14] Ultimately Dunlop, Abernathy, Hammond and Weil would conclude that the retail and apparel industries was undergoing technologically-driven changes every bit as revolutionary as those which had transformed the communication and transportation industries.

TRANSFORMATION IN ACTION

It was still dark in Boston's Downtown Crossing when Weil, Dunlop, Abernathy and Hammond showed up at 4AM to watch the trucks delivering goods to Macy's. Located in the site of the historic Filene's store that had towered over Boston's retail hub since 1912, Macy's was emblematic of the changes that were remaking the industry. Once the largest department store in the country, the Downtown Crossing store, like others in cities around the country, was now waging a losing battle against suburban competitors and "lean retailers" like Walmart. In the 1960's and 70's, the majority of apparel sales occurred in department stores. By the 1990's, that number had dropped to under thirty percent. In the late 1980's and early 1990's, such big name department stores as Saks Fifth Avenue, Gimbal's and Macy's had filed for bankruptcy. While the historic Filene's structure, designed by famed Chicago architect Daniel Burnham, appeared much the same from the outside, the department store it now housed was significantly weakened after rounds of mergers and corporate restructuring.[15]

Historically, retailing in the US had been an industry in which stores built inventory over time, based largely on guesswork about what items would sell. Retailers held onto their inventory, and what didn't move was discounted until it did. Perhaps no single store embodied this approach better than Boston's Filene's, where unsold items of clothing from the store's upper floors would eventually end up in the legendary Basement, the physical manifestation of guesswork gone wrong. By the 1990's however, big department stores had moved in a much "leaner" direction. The trucks that Weil and Dunlop and the others had come to downtown Boston to observe would once have contained single-order, long lead-time deliveries. Now the orders being transported from distribution centers to Macy's parent, Federated Department Stores, had been placed just days before, and reflected real-time customer demand rather than the intuition of buyers. What was more, the garments being delivered reflected a significant shift in the dynamics of customer demand and manufacturing practice. The long-lead items at the top of what the researchers described as the fashion triangle, represented an ever-shrinking share of the apparel market. Instead, the future was in so-called fashion basic items with short product cycles. Contained within those trucks idling outside of Macy was the entire story of growing product diversity and sped-up production, all fueled by customers hungry for variety.

At the center of this story was the inventory control that stores now had, "something they hadn't had before," says Abernathy.[16] He describes the inventory process at the Harvard Coop, for example, in which a representative of the Arrow Shirt Company would visit the story to determine what shirts were still in stock. While the store knew how many shirts had been sold, its knowledge stopped there, says Abernathy. "The Arrow guy would look and he'd say, 'well, 15 inch collar, 35 inch sleeve, they're out of that,' and he would then place an order with the company to make more of them."[17] Barcodes, which had already been widely adapted in grocery stores and were now being used at the point of sale in department stores, would transform inventory control across the apparel industry. Behind each pattern of machine readable data was a garment's entire history: the company that made it, its size and design specifics, down to when and where it was made. "It was barcodes that revolutionized things," says Abernathy.[18]

As the HCTAR team was beginning to understand, though, the transformation playing out in the stockrooms and the sales floors extended throughout the supply process. Their early morning visit to witness the trucks making deliveries to Macy's was just one stop along the supply chain. They began to work their way back through the chain, from a distribution center in Secaucus, NJ, to apparel operations and sewing factories, to textile production. At each stop, they gained a deeper understanding of the technology, processes and organization of the various enterprises, and more importantly, their increasing interdependence. The close-up look at the various facets of apparel and textile production was among the most instructive of the entire project, and took them far afield. "We would be going to textile plans in Jackson, Mississippi in the middle of the summer," says Weil. Dunlop was in his 80's by then, he notes, but it didn't matter.[19]

The researchers knew that they were onto something big. As their scope of inquiry widened, the project grew, becoming more ambitious. Dunlop, Weil, Abernathy and Hammond began to publish academic papers on the changing nature of inventory control. Their work would form the basis of the co-written study, *A Stitch in Time*. Staff members and researchers at HCTAR were tasked with bringing together industry leaders, garment union representatives and academics from across the country. A research relationship was established between with the Chinese Textile University in Shanghai to study the apparel and textile industries, including producing case studies of particular plants. Meanwhile, mounds of data were being collected, much of it in response to the team's extensive questionnaire that had been designed to solicit detailed information from apparel business units about their relationships with textile and retail organizations. "It got quite big," says Weil. "It was an amazing time to be studying these fundamental changes because they were really just starting."[20]

The HCTAR undertaking was of unusual breadth, even by Dunlop's standards. Yet in significant ways it was representative of his broader approach. The spirit that animated the entire enterprise was one of relentless questioning, each query giving rise to another until what resulted was the analysis of an entire system. "John always wanted to know how things fit together," says Weil. "How do the different forces in whatever institution you're trying to deal with lead to a set of outcomes?"[21] Dunlop's way of gaining a deep understanding of a system, whether it was industrial relations, the apparel and textile industries, or housing, which he would take on next, was through a very particular style of inquiry. "John was just very masterful at asking question after question to help you understand why things happened the way they did, and how did it ultimately help you understand the problem on the table," says Weil.[22]

Weil maintains that Dunlop approached all of the institutional problems he encountered as an economist. And yet even as his field of study and expertise provided him with a set of tools and a framework with which to view the world, Dunlop had little patience for academic economists, whom he regarded as hopelessly ivory tower. These he would take apart, says Weil, slamming the seminar table and exhorting students and fellow faculty members to learn the way the world works. Of course, there were worse disciplines than economics, like any discipline *besides* economics. "If he was in a sociology seminar, he's say 'you people have got to learn to think more like economists.'" Economics was his foundational tool, "but he went far beyond that," says Weil.[23]

Dunlop's inherent interest in how the pieces of a system or an institution fit together extended down to a granular level, to the individual relationships within an organization. Looking at an organization chart told you little about how an organization works, Dunlop would insist. "You got to understand how it really works by understanding the relationships in an institution. The only way you can do that is to listen, and talk and watch," says Weil.[24] In Dunlop's parlance, a key part of this process was 'casing the joint.' Explains Weil: "That meant figuring out who reported to who. Who was the power player? Who was the person with the information? Who was the person who would take the credit but actually wasn't really the decision maker?" A keen ability to listen, discerning the distinct perspectives of multiple people, was only part of what made Dunlop so effective, says Weil. "He was an incredible listener and he would probe in subtle ways about who was who, because that's the institutional take he had."[25] Paired with his perceptiveness was an ability to persuade people, to push them—sometimes indiscernibly, so that that they didn't realize they were being pushed at all, sometimes forcefully so that they ended up in whatever place Dunlop had had in mind all along.

Then there were Dunlop's particular habits of work, each aligned with his larger methodological approach. Before one could 'case the joint,' for example, it was necessary to get to the meeting site on time. "You had to arrive exactly three or four minutes early," recounts Abernathy. "Never late, but no earlier or they'll resent you because they had plans and a certain amount of work they were hoping to get done."[26] On a trip to San Francisco with Abernathy to visit the headquarters of Levi Strauss, Dunlop insisted on walking to their destination the night before so that he could time their arrival down to the exact minute. And while Dunlop was legendary for favoring the cheapest accommodations in town—it was said that wherever he stayed, the wrecking ball couldn't be far behind—this trip featured far more luxe digs than usual, thanks to Dunlop's old friend George Shultz. "I had two fireplaces and John had only one," recalls Abernathy. "I said 'look at this John!' He said he had more windows than I had."[27]

There was even a correct way to attend a cocktail party, as Weil learned while on a visit to Washington DC with Dunlop. When Weil appeared at their designated post-party meeting place ten minutes later than they'd arranged, Dunlop chastised him. "He looked at me and said 'David, you have to learn how to operate in a cocktail party setting.'"[28] There was a principle, as Weil was about to learn, and it involved a high degree of time management—two minutes per person to be precise. As Dunlop explained, moving around the room in a counterclockwise direction enabled him to arrive at the exit at the precise predetermined moment. Weil found these instructions amusing, but also revealing about Dunlop's style of work. A cocktail party was something to be approached with a clear vision and sense of purpose. "You're working the room and you're figuring out who you need to talk to, and all of this is about being very present and conscious about the pieces, and what you're trying to do," says Weil.[29] Even a room full of people drinking cocktails was to Dunlop a constellation of relationships and institutions, all embedded in a larger system.

CHANNELING CHANGE

"I hope you don't mind. I got itchy fingers on the weekend and I have a draft of a chapter," Dunlop told Abernathy.[30] The team was hard at work on *A Stitch in Time*, the publication of which would mark the culmination of the HCTAR project. The volume reflects the contributions and unique perspectives of its four authors, but at its core it is a fundamentally Dunlopian work. Revisit Dunlop's commentary for the revised version of his 1958 treatise on industrial relations, and it's easy to imagine that *A Stitch in Time* is just the sort of rejoinder to a labor economics that he saw as hopelessly divorced from the real world of industry. The volume begins with a sweeping tour of history—of retail and apparel manufacturing and sales—the hallmark of the industrial relations theorist's insistence that contemporary developments can't be understood without the lens of what preceded them. But then it ventures emphatically into the 'real world,' down to the view through the needle in the cutting room floor, plant work flow and the three types of spinning used to produce yarn.

Above all, *A Stitch in Time* reflects Dunlop's profound impatience with academia and its tolerance for the insular exchange of untested ideas. This was a book meant, not just to build understanding of a complex topic, but to influence the debate and change "habits, minds and thought patterns." Dunlop, Abernathy and the other researchers had taken on the task first presented to them by the Alfred P. Sloan Foundation, to analyze what was widely regarded to be a 'sunset industry,' and had come up with an entirely new way of thinking about the fundamental economic changes and challenges confronting apparel and textile manufacturing. Their trip through the supply chain led them to conclude that the widespread adoption of so-called 'lean retailing' didn't mean doom for the apparel and textile industries but in fact provided new opportunities—at least for some of them. By investing in information technology and changing their methods of planning and production, manufacturers were able to significantly reduce the amount of inventory they held, meaning that they no longer had to mark down or write off unsold products at the end of the year. Manufacturers that had reorganized their enterprises along these lines were twice as profitable as their traditional competitors—and not because they were paying their workers less or relying entirely on global sourcing. They *thought* differently, the researchers concluded, and that had major implications for other US industries.

The HCTAR collaboration would continue to bear fruit even after the team had completed its work on the official project. Abernathy expanded his work on inventory control, searching for ways to provide retailers with additional point-of-sale information so as to reduce their inventory risk. Janice Hammond would further the study of 'channel' coordination in the apparel and textile sectors that the HCTAR researchers had begun. Weil would expand his research on labor regulation well beyond the apparel and textile industries, to what he called the "fissured workplace," a supply chain grown ever longer, more fragmented and beyond the ability of workers and their organizations to influence it. Dunlop, meanwhile, was already thinking about other industries that might benefit from the application of the kind of systems lens that had proven so enlightening for the HCTAR project. Next up was housing, an industry that was historically very fragmented and prone to high rates of business failure, while also slow to adopt the kinds of innovations that had transformed other industries. Dunlop, Abernathy and Weil joined forces with two professors at Harvard's Joint Center for Housing Studies to look at ways of making residential home building more efficient.

Dunlop approached Abernathy because, as his long-time colleague liked to say, "I was the only engineer he knew."[31] As for Weil, he and Dunlop had formed a bond during their years of examining the retail/apparel supply chain—one that would grow deeper in the last years of Dunlop's life. When Weil had first begun working on the project, he was a new faculty member at Boston University's School of Management. But while BU was his official employer, Weil's base of operations was increasingly Harvard. That time spent in close proximity to Dunlop was vitally important to his own development, says Weil. "It gave me an active time to see John in action."[32] In their time together, whether driving from Belmont to Cambridge, or traveling to Washington DC or to some far-flung textile factory, they would discuss the problems that interested them both. Dunlop described how he had negotiated an end to the hostilities between Campbell Soup and the farmworkers who picked tomatoes for the company, background that would prove very useful for Weil when he took over that project after his mentor's death. "John was building that tripartite structure and I would hear all about that." Weil's favorite times, though, were when he could get Dunlop talking about history. "I used to love to get him to talk about riding the railroad with John L. Lewis."[33]

For Weil, the time he spent with Dunlop was also an affirmation that it was possible to pursue a course of life and work that wasn't just cross disciplinary but melded different worlds. Weil recalls that, growing up, it used to drive him crazy when his parents and grandparents would predict that he had an academic future, announcing that: "David's going to be a professor." Says Weil: "I used to get virulently angry at that because I thought professors sat in their offices and wrote books and didn't do anything about the world. I loved to learn and study, but I also had a side of me that wanted to go out and do things."[34] While the world that Weil had grown up in was far different from that of Dunlop's, by temperament and inclination they were similar. Of all of Dunlop's protégés, it was Weil who followed a path most resembling his mentor's. When the Harvard Trade Union Program that Dunlop and Sumner Slichter had founded in the 1940's was left without a director, it was Weil who stepped in and ran it. He would also take over for Dunlop as the head of the Dunlop Commission, the dispute resolution forum set up for farmworkers, growers and producers, first in the Midwest, and then expanded into North Carolina. "I kind of inherited it, but I felt like I knew all about it because I'd heard endless discussions with John," says Weil.[35]

Weil also followed his mentor's path to the Department of Labor. Dunlop had been the first secretary of labor to take up residence in the department's expanded Washington headquarters when they were completed in 1975; forty years later, Weil would take an extended leave from his academic job to spend nearly three years in Washington. As the US Wage and Hour Administrator, Weil oversaw work on the update and expansion of overtime regulations. He says that the move from Boston University and Harvard to government made him far more aware of the extent to which Dunlop was shaped by the constraints of government, and a deep impatience with academia. "He had no time for academics who thought that all they had to do was come up with the great idea, and then the poor people around them should go and do it, and working in government makes you realize that that's a completely naive way of thinking about the way the world works," says Weil, "because it doesn't work that way."[36] For all of their countless hours spent discussing industrial relations, mediation and problem solving, it was only when he arrived at the Department of Labor that Weil really understood how much of Dunlop's way of doing business reflected his years spent working in or alongside government.

In the last years of Dunlop's life, Weil's role expanded beyond that of mentee or academic colleague. He saw the professor who had had such a profound influence upon him as often as he could, driving him to meetings on housing or to the Joint Labor Management Committee that Dunlop still chaired. Some days he would drop by Dunlop's Belmont house on the pretense of needing to talk to him about a paper they were co-authoring, but really just to check on him. Dunlop's health was increasingly precarious, and since his wife had died, he was living alone. When he needed assistance with something, it was often Weil he would turn to. Like when he needed a longer cord for his telephone so that he could make calls without having to go into his home office. Weil got him one and set it up for him, and later that day, his own phone rang. "It was John, and he said: 'I just wanted you to know that it worked.'" The call ended the way any phone conversation with Dunlop did, recalls Weil. "John never said goodbye. He just hung up. Bam! And that was it."[37]

By Dunlop's own ambitious measures, the HCTAR project, and the TC² endeavor that preceded it, likely fell short. The US textile and apparel industries continued their dramatic decline as ever cheaper imports overwhelmed even higher-end garments, while the textile workers union at whose behest Dunlop's rethinking of the industry had been conducted all but disappeared. And yet the projects stand as a testament to this 'non-academic' figure in action. Dunlop had set out to think deeply about, and offer up solutions to the challenges of globalization. Along the way, he helped to conceive of a new way to think about supply chains, insights that continue to shape our understanding of today's on-demand economy. The difference between what Dunlop referred to dismissively as "any problem a person can solve by getting out of bed in the morning" and the big problems that he preferred was that the latter involved "changing the habits, the minds and thought patterns" of people, whether government representatives, union leaders or managers.[38] In a storied career replete with examples of 'big problems,' Dunlop's attempt to reimagine the US apparel and textile industries was among the biggest.

NOTES

1. Roger Rosenblatt, *Coming Apart: A Memoir of the Harvard Wars of 1969*, (Boston: Little, Brown, 1997) 113.
2. George Shultz, "John Dunlop," *Proceedings of the American Philosophical Society* 150, no. 1, (March 2006): 187–190.
3. David Weil, interviewed by the author, May 4, 2016.
4. Ibid.
5. Frederick Abernathy, interviewed by the author, June 23, 2016.
6. Ibid.
7. As Dunlop details in *Dispute Resolution: Negotiation and Consensus Building,* TC² was but one component of a multi-pronged project developed with the Amalgamated Clothing and Textile Workers Union beginning in 1976 and aimed at helping the ACTWU survive in an era of increased imports. Dunlop recommended that the ACTWU develop a joint training program, pursue government funding for an improved production process, and conduct genuine research and development. The experiment with roboticization would be at the center of the latter.

8. John T. Dunlop, *Dispute Resolution: Negotiation and Consensus Building* (Dover, MA: Auburn House Publishing, 1984), 248–249.
9. Ibid, 251.
10. By 1984, the budget for TC^2 was $2.65 million, reflecting both increased industry contributions and the Department of Commerce earmark.
11. Weil interview.
12. Ibid.
13. Even the survey was conducted via a collaborative approach. As Abernathy noted in his remarks at Dunlop's memorial service in 2003, retailers encouraged suppliers to fill out the survey, resulting in an unusually high completion rate.
14. Frederick Abernathy, John Dunlop, Janice Hammond and David Weil, *A Stitch in Time* (Oxford: Oxford University Press, 1999), viii.
15. Ibid, 49.
16. Abernathy interview.
17. Ibid.
18. Ibid.
19. Weil interview.
20. Ibid.
21. Ibid.
22. Ibid.
23. Ibid.
24. Ibid.
25. Ibid.
26. Abernathy interview.
27. Ibid.
28. Weil interview.
29. Ibid.
30. Abernathy interview.
31. Ibid.
32. Weil interview.
33. Ibid.
34. Ibid.
35. Ibid.
36. Ibid.
37. Ibid.
38. Email correspondence with Kris Rondeau, December 11, 2016.

Chapter Nine

A Union at Harvard

Harvard University, Dunlop's academic home beginning in 1939, was also the focus of some of his most consequential problem-solving work. In 1969, he had helped knit the university he loved back together after political strife threatened to pull it apart. Two decades later, he would play a similar role, working behind the scenes to craft a permanent resolution to the long-running strife between Harvard and the thousands of employees who made the university work. The first collective bargaining agreement between Harvard and its new union of clerical and technical workers, which Dunlop would negotiate on behalf of the university, was just one of many "institutional innovations" he would push for. And its implications would be felt far beyond Cambridge. Dunlop pointed to the union organizing effort and the unusual bargaining process that resulted from it as a model for another institution he'd often noted was not readily changed: organized labor.

If the results of Dunlop's handiwork are indisputable—the innovative labor agreement with its emphasis on employee decision making and joint labor/management dispute resolution remains in effect today—the origins of his involvement are somewhat less clear. The official version of events, presented in John Hoerr's book, *We Can't Eat Prestige*, is that Harvard economist Richard Freeman set things in motion by introducing Dunlop to the woman behind the years-long effort to unionize Harvard: Kris Rondeau. According to this account, Freeman spotted Rondeau in Harvard Square in the summer of 1987 and was concerned that the protracted union battle was taking a toll on her. "I tried to think of some way I could help her," recalls Freeman. His assistance came in the form of introducing Rondeau to his former professor and thesis advisor in hopes that Dunlop could help work out a "socially desirable solution" between the university and its employees.[1]

But Rondeau has a different version of events. As she recalls, she already knew Dunlop—at least she'd seen him around campus for years—and had heard him speak at various labor seminars. It was at one of these where the two would finally meet face to face, says Rondeau. The topic of this particular session was union organizing, and featured Charlie McDonald, then the AFL-CIO's director of organizing. As Rondeau recalls, she approached Dunlop at the end of the event. "I walked up to him and I said 'Professor Dunlop, I'm—'" And that was as far as she got. "He just turned around and started talking to somebody else." She would never discover the reason for this brusque reception—whether Dunlop didn't hear her, or if her appearance was to blame. "I looked like a scruffy kid," says Rondeau.[2]

Whatever the specifics of the backstory, their first official meeting took place in the late summer of 1987 at the Wursthaus, the famed Harvard Square eatery that functioned as Dunlop's unofficial office. "We were curious," Dunlop said to Rondeau by way of a greeting. "We wanted to know what we were dealing with."[3] Rondeau describes her reaction to this unusual welcome as both charmed and puzzled—she wasn't sure whether by 'we' Dunlop was referring to Harvard's president, Derek Bok, or to the royal "we." (It was the latter.) That inaugural meeting would set in motion a close friendship and collaboration that would last until Dunlop's death. Despite being separated by an age difference of nearly three decades, not to mention an institutional power divide, their connection was immediate, says Rondeau. "John always had an agenda and I always have an agenda, but more than anything our time together was fun."[4]

Rondeau soon joined the rotating cast of colleagues and associates with whom Dunlop met at his Wursthaus "office hours" each morning, kept afloat in gallons of the restaurant's coffee by a crew of servers who looked after him like a family member. During these regular morning meetings, Rondeau brought Dunlop up to speed about the state of the union organizing campaign, the fallout from the nasty break up between Harvard's nascent union and the United Auto Workers, the union with which the Harvard group was affiliated until 1985, and her conversations with American Federation of State, County and Municipal Employees, with which the union would ultimately affiliate. Dunlop, in turn, gave Rondeau a crash course in power dynamics at Harvard. "John felt like it was his responsibility to teach me about the university and how it worked and didn't work," recalls Rondeau. "I really thought Harvard was organized. I thought they had a plan, and that when they did something, they meant it. When I would say this to John, he would just laugh at me."[5]

IN SEARCH OF A VOICE

When Rondeau and Dunlop began meeting, the effort to organize the workers of Harvard had been underway in one form or another since the 1970's. Rondeau herself had gotten involved towards the end of the first union campaign, one that ended in 1977 when workers in Harvard's Medical Area voted against having a union. A second election, in 1981, had also resulted in a loss for the union. Now Rondeau and her crew of organizers were on the cusp of attempting a third election in which the entirety of Harvard's workforce—faculty secretaries, staff assistants, lab technicians, library and research assistants—would have the opportunity to decide on whether they wanted to be represented by the Harvard Union of Clerical and Technical Workers or HUCTW.

Much had changed since a handful of women had launched that initial bid to organize the Medical Area. The union, which had been affiliated with District 65 of the United Auto Workers, was now independent. Over the years, a distinct approach to organizing had emerged as well, one that centered gender at the heart of the effort to organize Harvard's overwhelmingly female workforce. In place of the antagonism that was the hallmark of traditional union organizing, Rondeau and her team emphasized one-on-one connections between organizers and university employees. And the demands had evolved as well, from the bread-and-butter focus on health care, or Harvard's notoriously low salaries for its female workers, to a broader emphasis on empowering the university's workers by giving them a voice in decision making. Rondeau would later describe the new union's approach this way: "We deserve to be there and can help them figure out solutions to problems. This is about power, participation, and self-representation."[6]

But while HUCTW may have evolved over time, Harvard had remained consistent in its resistance to the idea of its employees having a union. Rondeau had first experienced the university's anti-union campaign as a young lab worker, in the lead up to the 1981 election. During that period, the university had come at employees from all sides, deploying its anti-union message through letters and memos. But it was the small group meetings, in which Harvard administrators would call in between a half dozen and twenty Medical Area employees that Rondeau recalls as having a particularly chilling effect. "It was one of the most outrageously painful situations I'd ever seen and I was especially surprised at the willingness of the university to scare individuals and to have private conversations about their personal vulnerabilities," recalls Rondeau. "I was really appalled by it."[7]

Harvard's anti-union position was complicated by the fact that its president, Derek Bok, was a former teacher of labor law and had long written in favor of unions and the rights of workers to engage in collective bargaining. A contemporary and sometime collaborator with John Dunlop—the two co-authored a social history of the labor movement in 1970—Harvard's president was also the official administrative voice behind the anti-union campaigns. Indeed, he was the one who had authorized the campaigns, and though he'd insisted that administrators steer clear of intimidating tactics, it was his name that appeared on letters to employees urging them to vote against the union. On the day before the 1981 election, every Medical Area employee received a letter at home from President Bok, in which he explained that he was "not persuaded . . . that the choice of this union would be in your best interest."[8]

During the spring of 1988, with another election nearing, Harvard's anti-union tactics and Bok's particular role in facilitating them would become the subject of a campus-wide debate. Some 3,000 students signed onto a statement urging Harvard to remain neutral in the election campaign. Soon after, a group of 27 faculty members, including Harvard luminaries like Stephen Jay Gould, Laurence Tribe and Carol Gilligan, wrote their own letter criticizing the anti-union campaign. Civil rights, labor and religious groups sent representatives to meet with Bok, even holding a candlelight vigil outside his official university residence. President Bok was unmoved, however, and on the eve of the election, yet another letter was issued to every employee on campus, bearing the president's signature.

> I have always believed that it is a good thing for America and for working people that employees have the opportunity to vote for a union if they decide that their wages and working conditions will improve as a result. However, I am not at all persuaded in this case that union representation and collective bargaining will improve the working environment at Harvard or help us to sustain the highest quality of education and research.[9]

COERCIVE BALLOONS

The election was held on May 16th, 1988, and by the time the last votes were counted, the Harvard Union of Clerical and Technical Workers had won by the slimmest of margins. Of 3,400 eligible voters, 50.7 percent had voted in favor of having a union—just 44 more "yes" votes than "no's." "We were pretty surprised to win it," recalls Rondeau. "The university had put on quite an opposition, and there were a lot of factors that, had they not gone right for us, we would have lost by a hair's breadth."[10] Still, there wasn't much time to celebrate. The confetti had barely been swept up from Harvard's Memorial Hall, site of the vote count and an election night rally, before Harvard announced that the university wasn't done fighting.

A week later, Harvard would ask the National Labor Relations Board (NLRB) to overturn the election on the grounds that HUCTW had coerced employees into voting in favor of the union. How had this coercion taken place? In its complaint to the NLRB, Harvard alleged that the union had unduly influenced workers by "festooning" Harvard's campus with balloons and posters and by offering transport of pro-union voters to the polls. The university, which was represented by the Boston law firm Ropes and Gray, specialists in "union avoidance," claimed to have received complaints from more than 150 Harvard employees regarding intimidation or coercion. During the eight days of hearings, however, just 25 of these complainants would testify, and their accounts fell far short of either intimidation or coercion. "All they said was 'I saw balloons. I saw posters. They asked me if I had voted,'" recounts Rondeau. "After five or so of these experiences, I realized they had brought us there on a wild goose chase."[11]

It would take the NLRB judge months to review all the evidence and reach a decision. The announcement finally came during the lead up to a huge get-out-the-vote rally that HUCTW helped to organize for presidential candidate Michael Dukakis. Rondeau got word as she was walking into Sanders Theater for the big event. Not only had the NLRB ruled in favor of the union, but Jesse Jackson, who was headlining the rally, wanted to be the one to make the announcement to the packed house. "He talked about how in these dark times, there was a ray of hope in Cambridge, that we'd won the election, and people just went wild," recalls Rondeau.[12] Five months after the union vote, the victory was finally official. Harvard's clerical and technical workers had a union.

BEHIND THE SCENES

The judge's ruling, one that was critical of Harvard's lawyers to the point of censure, left Harvard with a difficult decision—and a deadline. Harvard administrators had 11 days to decide whether they were going to fight on or recognize the union. Continuing to fight the union after the election victory meant that the greatest university in the world would be embracing union busting, a point being made by a growing roster of critics. And yet key Harvard leaders were convinced that the university should continue to oppose the union.

"I was being urged by various people to fight to protest the union victory, which was quite narrow," recalls Derek Bok. "But then we got a negative ruling that upheld the union, and at that point, the question was, do we appeal that?"[13] While Bok's was the most prominent name attached to Harvard's anti-union efforts, he says that he was all too aware of the risks Harvard faced by fighting on. "We were running a risk that we would create an adversarial relationship with the union, that we might go the same way as Yale."[14] Yale, where campus workers had organized decades earlier, had seen bitter labor strife, including multiple strikes by unionized employees on campus.

The ultimate decision of which way to go rested in Bok's hands, and he consulted with John Dunlop to help him make it. As Rondeau recalls, Dunlop played no official role during the long lead-up to the election, or the tense post-victory period. In fact, his official position on Harvard's union problem seems to have been no position. His name didn't appear on the letter signed by 27 Harvard faculty on the eve of the election, demanding that the university stay out of the organizing effort. Nor did he pressure Bok to embrace the union, or at least deter from fighting the effort. But behind the scenes Dunlop was playing an increasingly instrumental role, says Rondeau. "He understood that this was a big mess that had to be cleaned up."[15]

And the situation at Harvard *was* a mess. Emboldened by its election victory and by the NLRB decision, HUCTW had stepped up its campaign to pressure Harvard into recognizing the union. Every night, union volunteers worked the phones, calling the university's donors and telling them about how Harvard treated its workers. Says Rondeau: "We'd been trying to win for so long, there was no turning back, and it just got bigger and bigger. We were in every aspect of the university's blood."[16]

Just as in 1969, when he'd been instrumental in helping the university negotiate the aftermath of the student strike, Dunlop saw the increasingly bitter battle between Harvard and its union as one that could destroy the institution he cared so much about. "He saw a disaster coming that in a lot of ways Harvard had created," says Rondeau.[17]

Still, when Bok consulted Dunlop during the tense period after the NLRB ruling, Dunlop didn't specifically advise him on whether Harvard should press forward with a legal case against the union. Instead, he proffered some practical advice to Bok: that should Harvard decide to recognize HUCTW, the administration might consider a sixty-day transition period before starting formal contract bargaining. As Dunlop explained, even a relatively brief "cooling off" period could go a long way towards helping dial back the rancor that had resulted from nearly a decade and a half of battles between the university and union supporters. Such a transition period might also help Harvard avoid the strife—and the strikes—that Yale had experienced, the result of an adversarial union election, immediately followed by adversarial contract negotiations.[18]

Dunlop also suggested that Bok meet with Kris Rondeau. During the lead up to the election and its aftermath, Dunlop and Bok had had several discussions about the nature of the union's leadership, and the woman with whom Dunlop had struck up an unusual friendship. "I knew John had grandfatherly affection for this young free-thinking union president," recalls Bok.[19] Rondeau didn't need much convincing either. When she received a surprise message from the staff at a hotel where she was conducting an organizing training south of Boston, instructing her to "call Derek Bok," she recognized Dunlop's handiwork immediately.[20] Their meeting, at Bok's Massachusetts Hall office on an October Saturday, would turn out to be the first of many.

Bok's conversations with Rondeau during this time seem to indicate that he was leaning towards recognizing the union—and that Dunlop's behind-the-scenes influence was having an effect. Bok presented Rondeau with Dunlop's transition idea, which she approved, having cleared it with the rest of her HUCTW crew. Officially, however, no decision had been made, even as the NLRB's November 4th deadline was rapidly approaching. "I imagine that Derek was probably being acted upon by a lot of people," recalls Rondeau, adding that she sensed that Bok was eager to put the fighting behind him. "John loved conflict, but I don't think Derek loved conflict."[21]

Rondeau's instincts proved to be correct. On November 4th, despite having gotten a five-day extension from the NLRB, Bok made a surprise announcement: Harvard would recognize the union. His decision meant that he'd overruled Harvard's lawyers as well as the university's outside attorneys from Ropes and Grey, all of whom remained convinced that Harvard had the legal case to push on. He had also gone against a number of powerful university administrators who were committed to continuing the fight against the union, including deans who held outsized sway within Harvard's decentralized system.[22]

Ultimately Bok took the position that Dunlop had been pushing for: recognition of the union followed by a transition period. But if Dunlop had succeeded in helping win a short-term solution to Harvard's battles with the union, the real work of long-term problem solving was just getting started. "We'll make it work," read the buttons that university administrators handed around after Bok's announcement.[23] All that remained was to figure out what that meant.

WE'LL MAKE IT WORK

"The president of the university decided that we should negotiate with this union and he wrapped up all this lovely past in a bundle and threw it me and said it's your job," was how Dunlop described Bok's decision to entrust him with the job of bargaining with Harvard's new union.[24] But in many ways, Dunlop was the logical choice to lead the university through what was certain to be a dramatic change in the way that it conducted labor relations. He came from outside of the administration, which was important to Rondeau, but had the kind of insider credentials that came from three decades of serving Harvard, including in the capacity of Dean of the Faculty of Arts and Sciences from 1970–1973. Nor was there anyone else at Harvard who could claim his level of experience untangling complex labor disputes. When Bok tapped him to negotiate a first contract between Harvard and its employees, Dunlop was just wrapping up a successful resolution between Campbell Soup and the union representing thousands of migrant tomato and cucumber pickers in the Midwest.

But while Dunlop had been Rondeau's top choice, she still wasn't convinced that he understood how important gender had been to HUCTW's approach to organizing, and the union's ultimate success. "John didn't think about gender and I was all about gender," recalls Rondeau.[25] She wanted to make sure that Dunlop "got" that, just as HUCTW had eschewed traditional adversarial-style organizing in favor of deeper one-on-one connections, the union had every intention of imprinting its unique style on negotiating and dealing with the university. In other words, this was going to be a style of labor relations like Dunlop had never seen before. "I said to him: 'I need you to know this. You're not dealing with Lane or Tommy. You're not dealing Jerry McEntee or any of those boys. You're dealing with me,'" recalls Rondeau.[26]

For Rondeau that meant establishing a structure for dialogue with the university that would allow the union to make real the vision of unionism that she and other organizers had been articulating for years. If Harvard employees had elected to have a union in order to have a greater voice in decision making, then the process of negotiating with Harvard needed to reflect that. Rondeau wanted to break with traditional bargaining by including lots of people, something that, as she argued, would have the additional benefit of providing union organizers and activists, almost all of whom were women, with the experience they'd need to lead. Dunlop didn't blink, recalls Rondeau. "He was interested in the women's aspect of the organizing."[27] Dunlop also shared Rondeau's commitment to a vision of unionism that went beyond traditional bread and butter issues to something that, as he said, "would give more meaning to the lives and careers . . . of people who are in this bargaining unit."[28]

The irony was that, on paper at least, Dunlop seemed to represent exactly the sort of Harvard power imbalance that the union campaign had been about. He was "one of them," the men who'd run Harvard forever. What made Dunlop different, says Rondeau, was that he not only thought about the long trail of secretaries who'd run his office and overseen his calendar—like Helen Knox, who accompanied him to Washington during his assorted "tours of duty," or Marie Stroud, who would work for him until he died—he had respect for them. "And you know, that's not true of a lot of Harvard faculty."[29]

Meshing philosophical approaches to labor relations and agreeing on the role that gender should play was only one set of challenges that Rondeau and Dunlop faced. The prospect of putting together a collective bargaining process was daunting. Harvard was known for being a decentralized system, the autonomy of its assorted schools and institutions summed up in a single saying: "every tub on its own bottom." "It was really an incredibly difficult problem," says Bok. "Separate faculties running separate institutions, bargaining that would cover all kinds of different jobs. And it wasn't a question of amending an existing agreement—we had to start from scratch."[30]

Dunlop suggested that Jim Healy join the team in the role of permanent facilitator. Healy, who was, like Dunlop, an emeritus professor of economics at Harvard, also had decades of experience handling often complex labor management negotiations. He'd played a similar facilitation role between the UAW and the Ford Motor Company, and Dunlop hoped that Healy would be able to step in and assist in order to keep the tricky bargaining process from breaking down. Both Rondeau and Bok approved of the choice, but for different reasons. Bok appreciated that a Harvard problem was going to be resolved in a Harvard way: by tapping the deep expertise of its faculty. "Of course, they rallied around the way Harvard faculty always do when the institution is really having trouble," recalls Bok.[31] For Rondeau's part, it was Healy's deep affinity for labor that was the attraction. While his forty-years plus as a mediator and negotiator commanded respect, he also had a unique ability to connect with workers—a combination that would prove essential in the difficult months ahead.

A SEAT AT THE TABLES

The ninety-day transition period played out much as Dunlop had anticipated, giving both sides a much-needed breather after years of tension and tumult. From the heated rhetoric of just a few months ago, Harvard and its new union, represented by two eight-member transition teams, were now engaged in weekly information exchanges. But the transition did more than just lower the temperature. It allowed for the creation of an unusual participatory structure through which official negotiations would be carried out—a top priority for Rondeau and her team. The cooling-off period also gave HUCTW an opportunity to demonstrate that all of its talk about collaborative problem solving wasn't just show. To deal with disputes that arose during the transition and subsequent negotiations, both sides designated two representatives to serve as part of a interregnum problem solving team "We said there are inevitably going to be problems that arise during the course of each day," Dunlop said, describing how he and Rondeau came up with the concept. "Let us agree to set up a problem-solving team of initially two on each side who apart from any agreement, because we don't yet have an agreement, will have the responsibility of trying to keep the peace in the interim while these discussions go forward."[32]

The transition talks wrapped up in mid-February, the parties having reached an understanding that welcomed HUCTW into the university's governance process. Now it was time to bargain. At the center of the bargaining process were nine "tables," formal bodies set up to deal with key issues including salary and job classification, pensions, health and safety, affirmative action and employee participation. Sixty-five union members, who'd been elected by their peers, served as HUCTW's bargaining representatives, bringing with them suggestions that had been solicited from the broader membership. This large group was then subdivided into negotiating tables by issue: salary, pensions, health care, career development, work and family, voice and participation. On the university side, faculty members and four dozen administrators, including deans, participated in the tables.[33] Explained Dunlop: "That had the great merit of permitting a great many people in the union to get acquainted with a great many people on the management side and find out they all didn't have horns."[34]

Communication was constant, both within the teams and between the opposing sides. On one weeknight, the entire union team would meet. Then the next night, the assorted union tables would meet. Then each table would meet with its management counterparts. Instead of the typical adversarial back-and-forth that characterized traditional collective bargaining, this was conversation aimed at defining mutual interests and objectives and identifying areas of potential conflict. Only after a shared understanding was reached would the bargaining teams move onto specific proposals. And such was the commitment to maintaining a non-adversarial climate that lawyers were entirely excluded from the process.[35]

For Harvard's secretaries, who'd never had a voice before, this was a big deal, says Rondeau. Suddenly they had a seat at the table, meeting on equal footing with the very same Harvard administrators who held such power over them. "We'd written about this style of unionism and how we saw the world. There was a tone to it and the university kept saying 'we don't believe it,'" recalls Rondeau. "Nobody in the university believed it except for maybe John Dunlop."[36]

From his office in Massachusetts Hall, Derek Bok took note of the process with a sense of relief—Harvard had avoided, thus far at least, the fate of either Yale, or Boston University, where contract negotiations broke down, resulting in strikes. And he admired the way that his two Harvard experts, Dunlop and Healy, had worked with Rondeau to solve an immensely challenging problem. "They spent an enormous amount of time organizing this complicated system of tables that were in charge of different parts of the agreement," recalls Bok. "It was a pleasure to watch."[37]

For all the complexity of the process, the negotiations moved along rapidly. For Rondeau and her crew, the intensity of the transition period and bargaining wasn't much of a departure from the speed at which they'd been working for years. But the tight timeline also represented a prerogative for Dunlop. "John wanted to be done by graduation," recalls Rondeau.[38] Now that the hard work of getting the parties to the table, or tables in this case, had been done, the goal was quick action, spurred not just by the parties' shared understanding of a common goal, but a sense of momentum from the process itself.[39] Meanwhile, the union kept up the pressure that had brought the university to the table in the first place, holding rallies and other campaign events.

DONE DEAL

The teams wrapped up their work at the beginning of June. Rondeau and Dunlop then spent the next several weeks meeting with members of their respective communities, explaining the prospective deal. While a collective bargaining agreement was brand new territory for Harvard, this was an unusual contract by any standard. For one thing, it relied extensively on joint labor-management teams, not just to solve problems and resolve disputes, but with an eye towards fundamentally reshaping the relationship between Harvard and its employees. Joint committees were proposed in each school for a variety of key areas, including health and safety, affirmative action, family policy and a reworking of the university's job classification system.

This was more than a tentative deal between an institution and its union negotiating partner. Dunlop and Rondeau and their respective teams had essentially crafted a new governing structure for the university. The emphasis on employee voice and participation reflected Rondeau's vision and represented the logical extension of HUCTW's non-adversarial approach to unionism. For his part, Dunlop made the case to his colleagues, including the deans and administrators who'd spent years resisting the union, that the agreement's emphasis on joint councils for decision making and dispute resolution made sense for an organization as loosely organized as Harvard was. "I think that it is particularly appropriate in a highly decentralized university," Dunlop told the *Harvard Crimson* in an interview, citing the different priorities and rules in each of Harvard's largely autonomous units. "The alternate approach to a joint council is to have very much more-detailed rules in the master agreement."[40]

There were also plenty of "bread-and-butter" gains for Harvard's employees in the proposed agreement, including pensions, health and dental insurance, and a substantial wage hike. Here Rondeau would have a far easier time making the case for the deal to her community than Dunlop would to his. When he took the agreement to Derek Bok for review, the president balked at the size of the compensation increase. "I said 'John, I can't settle with this. The deans will go up in smoke. I've got to show my deans and my governing boards that we're not going to bankrupt the place,'" Bok recalls. "Good trooper" that Harvard's chief negotiator was, says Bok, Dunlop then went back to the union with the message that there was no way that Harvard would approve such a substantial wage hike.[41]

The final agreement, officially reached on June 25, 1989 and ratified by 94 percent of the union membership soon after, contained a wage hike that would boost the average Harvard employee's pay by more than one third over the course of three years.[42] In other words, the deal was not as rich as it had been, but it still represented a major advance, says Rondeau. "I'm sure that if you were a Harvard dean you would think the agreement was too rich. But the truth was that our wages were horribly low, and they needed this kind of boost in order to begin to make middle class jobs out of this kind of work."[43]

LOOKING BACK

Nearly four decades have passed since Harvard employees voted to become part of a union. And while the nature of the union's work has shifted in that time, from organizing a vast workforce to managing the benefits of one, the governance framework that Dunlop helped to implement remains largely intact. That is not to say that there haven't been periods of tension and strife, the worst of which occurred in 1992, when Derek Bok stepped down as president of Harvard and was replaced by Neil Rudenstein. Dunlop was removed from his role as chief negotiator amid persistent rumblings that he had "given away the store," recalls Rondeau. "The idea was not to bargain with the union. It was like having the whole union drive again."[44] Seventy-three events later, including a huge rally headlined by Jesse Jackson, Harvard and HUCTW would settle their second contract.

Now long retired from the presidency, Derek Bok has come to believe that having a union has ultimately been a good thing for Harvard. "It has cost a fair amount of money but I think it has probably improved the quality of the relationship," Bok says. Reflecting on the relationship between Harvard and its union, Bok strikes a far different tone than the university president whose name once appeared on anti-union letters to employees. "It does teach me that however benevolent you think you are, if you don't have somebody looking out for some big constituency, you probably don't do as much for their legitimate interests as you should," says Bok.[45]

As for his decision to call upon John Dunlop to once more help mend the institution he loved, and which, like in 1969, stood in danger of coming apart, Bok remains convinced that his choice was essential. "Deep down John loved Harvard. I think that's what made him so mad when he thought the university was behaving irresponsibly." His love for Harvard made him determined, not just to fix the university's mess, says Bok, but to put the relationship with the union on a cooperative and constructive path. "That was clearly John's doing."[46]

Bok's mind wasn't the only one changed through the course of Harvard's dealings with its biggest union. Dunlop too became a convert to a different way of organizing, and to the merits of opening up union negotiations to a broader swath of the membership than was typical. A believer in the power, indeed, the necessity, of persuasion as a way of reaching meaningful compromise between parties, Dunlop would end up persuaded that participation could be a tool in the problem-solving process. In a joint presentation with Rondeau in 1990, the famously taciturn Dunlop was as passionate an emissary for HUCTW's style of union-organizing-as-relationship-building as Rondeau herself.

Dunlop pointed with particular pride to the statement that the problem-solving team had crafted, prior to the start of negotiations, illustrating the spirit with which the enterprise was being conducted. Harvard had come to be governed through a cooperative process among governing boards and administrators, faculty, students and alumni. That was history, said Dunlop. Now was the time to welcome the support staff in libraries and laboratories and in academic and administrative officers and senders, represented by HUCTW as a valued and essential participant in this process.[47] And just like he had two decades before, Dunlop used the challenge with which he'd been presented to try to nudge Harvard into the future. The participatory structure of the union, coupled with the unique approach to negotiations, had given voice to thousands of employees who'd long lacked a say on the job. To the famously closed institution, Dunlop, Rondeau and their respective colleagues had brought participation at every level. "That at least is our combined objective," noted Dunlop.[48]

NOTES

1. John Hoerr, *We Can't Eat Prestige: The Women Who Organized Harvard*, (Philadelphia: Temple University Press, 1997) 218.
2. Kris Rondeau, interviewed by the author, March 15, 2016.
3. Ibid.
4. Ibid.
5. Ibid.
6. Kris Rondeau, cited in "Harvard University Union, Management Have Working Relationship, Parties Say," *Labor Relations Week*, April 11, 1990, 357.
7. Rondeau interview.
8. Hoerr, 103.
9. Cited in Hoerr, 204.
10. Rondeau interview.
11. Cited in Hoerr, 214.
12. Rondeau interview.
13. Derek Bok, interviewed by the author, May 5, 2016

14. Ibid.
15. Rondeau interview.
16. Ibid.
17. Ibid.
18. Bok interview.
19. Ibid.
20. Rondeau interview.
21. Ibid.
22. Hoerr, 223–224.
23. Ibid.
24. Dunlop and Rondeau presentation, University of Arizona, June 27, 1990.
25. Rondeau interview.
26. Ibid.
27. Ibid.
28. Dunlop and Rondeau presentation.
29. Rondeau interview.
30. Bok interview.
31. Ibid.
32. Dunlop and Rondeau presentation.
33. Hoerr, 228.
34. Dunlop and Rondeau presentation.
35. Richard Hurd, "Organizing and Representing Clerical Workers: The Harvard Model," in Women and Unions, ed. Dorothy Sue Cobble, (Ithaca: ILR Press, 1993), 327.
36. Rondeau interview.
37. Bok interview.
38. Rondeau interview.
39. As Jonathan Brock describes in *Bargaining Beyond Impasse*, quick action is a key element that the labor/management dispute resolution approach that Dunlop developed.
40. Marion Gammill, "A Struggle for Empowerment," *Harvard Crimson*, May 19, 1993.
41. Bok interview.
42. Hurd, 327–328.
43. Rondeau interview.
44. Ibid.
45. Bok interview.
46. Ibid.
47. Dunlop and Rondeau presentation.
48. Ibid.

Chapter Ten

Joint Problem Solving

The genesis of the Joint Labor-Management Committee for Municipal Police and Fire Fighters (JLMC), what would become John Dunlop's longest-running problem-solving forum, arrived in the form of an unlikely phone call. In late summer of 1977, the City Manager for Cambridge, Massachusetts contacted Dunlop to ask if he would be willing to meet with some representatives of the fire fighters union and an organization representing Massachusetts cities and towns in order to "discuss a problem." As for the nature of the problem, no further information was given, recounts Jonathan Brock, in his detailed examination of the history and workings of the JLMC.[1] Intrigued, Dunlop invited the parties to have lunch with him at the Harvard Faculty Club, where they filled him in on the politically explosive issue of binding arbitration, which, despite intentions to stabilize labor relations and preclude the disruption of strikes, had led to highly contentious and damaging disputes between police and firefighters and Massachusetts cities and towns. Impressed by their willingness to work together to solve a difficult problem, Dunlop eagerly agreed to help them. And so instead of marking the end of that summer with a barbecue or a trip to the beach, Dunlop spent Labor Day weekend fashioning a "mechanism" aimed at ending decades of bitterness between Massachusetts' municipalities and their public servants.

When representatives of the Massachusetts Professional Fire Fighters and the Massachusetts League of Cities and Towns reached out to Dunlop, it was after a particularly acrimonious period in the brief history of public sector unions in the state. Not until 1958 were public employees in the Bay State afforded the right to join unions. As in 32 other states, such employees were forbidden from striking, which meant that they had no way to force management to move on contract disputes, some of which dragged on for years. The search for a stronger tool to resolve disputes led the unions to push for so-called last-best-offer arbitration. In 1974, over the objections of municipal leaders, the League of Cities and Towns and an anti-tax group, legislation giving police and fire fighters last-best-offer arbitration squeaked through the Statehouse. But while the legislation's passage represented an important victory for the public safety unions, opposition to final arbitration would only deepen in the next few years.

In theory, last-best-offer arbitration was supposed to improve collective bargaining. Under the style chosen by Massachusetts in 1973, both sides submitted their positions, and the arbitrator chose one, unlike conventional arbitration in which the arbitrator fashioned his or her own award. The argument behind the approach was that it forces the parties to try to reach accommodation. The motivation, as Brock explains, "is that the threat of having to accept for settlement the position tendered by the other side would be so repugnant that it would force the parties to seek to accommodate their differences."[2] The reality fell far short of this, however. Because management, in this case municipal authorities, resented having a third party tell them how to spend their money, the foot-dragging that had spurred police and fire fighters to push for last-best-offer arbitration in the first place dragged on. Such endless delays served to poison relationships between labor and management, making problem solving and dispute resolution all the more difficult. The lack of clarity over the future of the statute itself also worked as a deterrent against collective bargaining as the parties waited for the myriad legislative battles to play out.

Politics made for an even more combustible mix. Mayors had a political incentive to blame settlements on an arbitrator rather than take the blame for raises, while union leaders were under pressure to demonstrate to their members that they were fighting hard for them. These parallel political incentives seemed to be as great as the fear of the other side's proposal being imposed, recalls Brock.[3] With both sides effectively rewarded for taking extreme positions, bargaining and solving problems often took a backseat to political posturing.

While the arguments for and against last-best-offer arbitration were playing out on Beacon Hill and in the pages of the *Boston Globe*, another intense debate was taking shape across the country over taxes. A consequence of the severe inflation of the 1970's that Dunlop had spent so much of his career in government trying to control was that property taxes were soaring. In California, this spike in property taxes would spur a backlash that resulted in the passage of Proposition 13. While Proposition 2 ½, the Massachusetts' anti-tax measure, wouldn't pass until 1980, opposition to the state's relatively high level of taxation was strong and growing stronger. When municipal officials pointed to what they saw as outsized settlements for police and fire unions during the three years of the state's experiment with last-best-offer arbitration, their warnings resonated with a populace grown weary of high taxes. The unions, which wanted to see the arbitration measure made permanent, had the political heft needed to get an extension passed in the legislature, and the votes to override Governor Dukakis' veto. But local officials revolted, and the Massachusetts League of Cities and Towns announced plans to take the issue to the people in the form of a ballot referendum.

It had been a year and a half since Dunlop had handed in his resignation to President Ford. While still traveling back and forth to Washington for meetings of the Labor-Management Committee, Harvard Business School was now his home base. He may have given up the impressive government title, but in labor circles he was something of a legend. "John Dunlop has left the Secretary of Labor's Job and he's back at Harvard. Maybe we should talk to him," John Jennings, the Secretary Treasurer of the statewide fire fighters association said at the time.[4] Such was Dunlop's reputation as a mediator and a problem solver that it extended well beyond the confines of the labor movement. The League of Cities and Towns, which represented the employers, in this case the municipal authorities that sat on the other side of the bargaining table, was convinced that Dunlop could help them too. Both groups were inspired by Dunlop's long experience bringing together labor and management in the interest of solving problems. "It was right up Dunlop's alley," says Jim Costello, a member of the Carpenter's union who would join the new commission as a staff member, a position he held for nearly four decades.[5]

The two sides brought with them something that Dunlop knew was key to any serious negotiations—the alternative to *not* hammering out a solution was worse. The unions were loathe to see the arbitration issue go to the ballot, as the municipal groups were threatening. Ballot fights were notoriously expensive, and the issue of binding arbitration was extremely complex, meaning that it didn't lend itself to the sort of slogans that made for winning campaigns. And limited as it was to police and fire unions, binding arbitration wasn't necessarily the kind of labor issue that would bring union members out in droves. A poll taken late in the summer of 1977 perfectly captured the union's dilemma, revealing that while the firefighters had overwhelming public support, the public also believed that they should have the opportunity to vote on public employee raises. Despite having public opinion in its corner, the League of Cities and Towns appeared doubtful about its abilities to gather enough signatures to get the arbitration question onto the ballot. Both sides "saw something to lose should the other side carry the issue," writes Brock. The recent political machinations were just the latest in a history marked by bitterness and rancor. Legislators, meanwhile, were caught in the middle, forced to choose between the taxpayers and municipalities they represented and the firefighters, whose numbers and organization gave them considerable strength on Beacon Hill.

For his part, Dunlop came away from his initial encounter with the representatives of the two sides feeling impressed. Demetrios Moschos, the assistant city manager of Worcester, who represented the League, and Randolph fire fighter Dusty Alward, representing the fire service, seemed to have a shared understanding of where precisely the problems in their relationship lay. More importantly, they'd come together in order to seek out some kind of compromise. He quickly recognized the opportunity to create a mechanism aimed, not just at solving the specific problem at hand but at establishing a new way to resolve public sector disputes. "He told us that interest arbitration is a failure of the collective bargaining process," recalls Moschos. "It's not a victory. The parties themselves should bargain to a satisfactory conclusion."[6] For Moschos, who had often assigned readings from Dunlop's treatise on industrial relations to his labor relations students at Worcester State College, Dunlop's words were transformative. "I've never forgotten what he said that first time that we met," says Moschos. "I have fond memories of those meetings at Harvard as we worked on the agreement."[7]

The memorandum of understanding that Dunlop crafted over Labor Day weekend in 1977 is a revealing document. It provided for the creation of a joint committee made up of officials representing both labor and management, as both sides had agreed to during their discussions at Harvard. While the agreement spelled out the details of how the new body would function, it also laid out a broad, even bold, vision of the rationale behind the creation of the problem-solving mechanism. Instead of dwelling upon the bitterness of the past and assuming a state of perpetual rancor, the memorandum assumed that both parties wanted to improve their relationship in order to better serve the public. Making collective bargaining less contentious and litigious would strengthen it, Dunlop wrote, and better enable the parties to seek out solutions that were both practical and equitable.[8] The crisis that had thrust the parties together became, in Dunlop's hands, an opportunity to better serve the public interest.

The parties approved Dunlop's agreement on September 19, 1977, but one more hurdle remained before the new committee could officially commence operations. While Dunlop drew on his extensive experience in private sector labor relations in shaping the new structure, its public nature meant that the legislature and the governor also had to approve it. Compared to the endless legislative battles over situs picketing and labor law reform that had taken up so much of Dunlop's time during his tour of duty at the Department of Labor, getting approval for the Joint Labor Management Committee would be a snap. The document authored by Dunlop was brought to the state legislature and the governor as a joint proposal by both sides, the statute authored by Moschos. As Brock notes, the symbol of the two sides coming together in agreement on a workable way to solve their problems was a powerful one. "[T]hese important political figures quickly agreed and resolved the political dilemma created by the intense battle for votes in the legislature and the problem of subsequent election support," writes Brock.[9] The bill passed largely as is and was signed by the governor. The new entity, sketched out by Dunlop over the course of a weekend, was official, and had wide-ranging authority to resolve police and firefighter disputes, thus avoiding binding arbitration.[10]

PROCESS AT WORK

When asked by Bruce Kaufman in his sweeping 2002 interview about what he regarded as his most significant contributions, Dunlop, after suggesting that he might not be the person to answer such a question objectively, conducted a brief tour of his career. He wrapped up his response with a mention of the "numerous dispute resolution systems in many industries I have helped to create and have administered."[11] While he doesn't mention the Joint Labor Management Committee by name, it stands as a significant representation of Dunlop's vision and approach. Starting from his deeply-held belief that the major obstacle to solving labor/management problems was the lack of a forum in which to hold open discussions, Dunlop drew upon the energy of the moment and the resolve of the parties and to create just such a forum. What's more, the manner in which Dunlop approached the problems at hand provides insight into his own creative process. By the time he sat down in his Belmont home office to draft a memorandum for the forum he envisioned, Dunlop had gained a deep understanding into virtually every aspect of public sector collective bargaining in Massachusetts. The mechanism he proposed was tailored both to respond to the specific conflict, but also to address what Dunlop saw as the need for long-term reform.

When the Joint Labor Management Committee officially came into being on January 1, 1978, it was made up of a total of 13 members. Six management members, mostly local officials, joined labor representatives, consisting of senior officers from the Professional Fire Fighters of Massachusetts, along with the two organizations representing police officers in Massachusetts. Moschos served as the management chair, while Captain Dusty Alward occupied the position of labor chair. As laid out in the statute, management representatives were to be nominated by a governor-appointed committee, while the labor seats were to be proposed by the three unions involved. The chairperson was to be nominated by the 12 committee members and presented to the governor, who was required by law to make the appointment.[12] And since the committee wouldn't exist without Dunlop, he was the obvious choice to serve as its chairperson, recalls Moschos. "We asked Dunlop since he was the father. At first he wasn't enthusiastic; he didn't want to be involved."[13] Moschos and Alward convinced him, however, and the JLMC had its first chair, or in the parlance of the mediator, its "strong neutral." "Once Dunlop got involved," says Moschos, "he got very enthusiastic and very interested and paid a lot of attention."[14]

The day to day work of the committee was done by a handful of paid staffers. Dunlop himself was paid on a per diem basis, while staffers representing labor and management worked with their respective parties; a part-time data analyst provided the essential information necessary for negotiations. The principals representing various unions and municipalities also received small stipends for their time. While many of them had jobs that included a labor-management relations component, the fact that they had full-time positions served as an inducement to seek expeditious resolutions. That Dunlop staple of negotiations, 'encouraging' compromise by keeping the various parties at the table until they couldn't take it anymore had a companion here.

Also important was the JLMC's independent status. Both sides viewed the Board of Conciliation and Arbitration (BCA), the state entity tasked with dispute resolution, as overly bureaucratic. Altering the nature of labor relations in Massachusetts, saw Dunlop, would require more than just tinkering with the existing rules under which the board operated. Recalls Moschos: "Dunlop said from the very beginning the key is the parties, not the government. The parties need to cooperate and take responsibility for their actions in order to move collective bargaining forward."[15] In keeping with Dunlop's long-standing preference, the committee was set up to be independent, "emphasizing informal accommodation rather than competitive legal proceedings."[16] Two staff representatives, one from labor, one from management, oversaw the work of the volunteer members and coordinated the committee's day to day work. The staff was small and flexible enough that even the administrator, tasked with setting up meetings, often found him or herself involved in helping work out disputes. A research person, meanwhile, typically a Harvard PhD student, was responsible for analyzing the committee's work, both for internal purposes and so that the JLMC could report on its progress to the legislature. And while the staff people may have been unaware of it, the structure of their work reflected yet another of Dunlop's mechanisms in operation. Just as his beloved committees enabled the exchange of diverse ideas, here, academics, union leaders, and municipal representatives, who typically ran in very separate circles, were constantly rubbing elbows and learning from one another. The academic researchers were thrust into the 'real world' with its politics and need for compromise. The union leaders, meanwhile, were pushed to think more broadly about their role, and the core services provided by their members.

Finally, the JLMC was built to weather internal differences that were rife within the municipal landscape, both on the municipal side and within the police and fire unions. "Finance committee members and selectman may often disagree; mayors and city councils may be at odds," wrote Dunlop in his 1984 volume, *Dispute Resolution: Negotiation and Consensus Building*.[17] Union elections were another complicating factor, especially when the contests spilled over into rival bargaining positions. The JLMC reflected this realpolitik in its very structure. "Because the business of government includes politics, the dispute resolution machinery must be able to operate effectively in such an environment," wrote Dunlop.[18]

CASE CLOSED

"I thought we straightened that out already!" Dunlop remarked with his customary impatience.[19] The JLMC was holding its weekly meeting, where staff members and field investigators gathered to discuss the status of various cases, Dunlop, the committee's chairman, firmly at the helm. His query was in regards to one of the JLMC's first cases: a bitter and years-long dispute between the town of Seabury, MA and its fire service. In many ways, the issues in Seabury were representative of just the sorts of problems that the JLMC had been created to solve: a long-running battle between the two sides, marked by personality and political clashes that made productive dialogue and progress all but impossible. Untangling the various tendrils of the dispute would require intensive work on the JLMC's part. Committee members, representing both labor and management, were dispatched to the scenic town to meet with selectmen and union negotiators. Meanwhile the chairman, who was deeply immersed in even the smallest details regarding the negotiating process, was prepared to step in should the two sides fail to reach an agreement.

Just three years before, Dunlop had been operating in a very different realm. As secretary of labor, he'd met with President Ford regularly and was engaged in round-the-clock negotiations over such delicate matters as selling wheat to the Soviets, not to mention the high-pressure work of trying to get situs picketing legislation passed. Now here he was engaged in the most local of disputes: the town of Seabury, MA vs its fire service, down to the details of which members of the negotiating team for the town were at war with the leadership of the union representatives. And yet as colleagues who worked with him during various phases of the Committee could attest, Dunlop was deeply engaged in its work. If he viewed this problem-solving venue as inferior to Capitol Hill, he gave no indication to that effect. "He really liked working on this. It was his committee and he was really proud of it," says Brock, who'd worked at the Cost of Living Council and the Department of Labor, both under Dunlop's tenure, and had had the opportunity to observe his problem-solving activities.[20] As the author of a study of the JLMC, Brock also had the opportunity to talk with Dunlop at length about how he viewed the enterprise.

Brock argues that in important ways the JLMC represented a culmination of Dunlop's dispute resolution work, enabling him to bring together many of the different approaches he'd used over the years. There was his reliance on committees, for example, with their divergent perspectives and expertise that Dunlop believed was absolutely key to understanding a particular problem and working towards a solution. "He had a committee structure through all of his projects," notes Brock. Now he had an opportunity to apply that structure to the problem of binding arbitration that existed in half of the states in the US. "He thought 'there's a big problem out there. Here's something I can do about it,'" says Brock. [21] Dunlop's close involvement with the committee meant that he got to refine its structure as it evolved, including coming up with new tools to add to his problem-solving arsenal.

Take the idea of sending "observers" to Seabury. In order to solve the long-running dispute there, the JLMC needed to untangle years of rancor. Dispatching mediators or an arbitrator to the scene likely wouldn't produce much, Dunlop knew, as these were likely to be perceived as threatening, even as the underlying problems that had caused collective bargaining to fray in the first place were left unsolved. "He always said that no arbitrator can really understand the parties' positions, and the parties still have to live with each other after the award," recalls Moschos.[22] Worse still were lawyers who had a financial interest in seeing disputes like the one between Seabury and its fire service drag on.

Dunlop circumvented both the arbitrators and the lawyers, hatching a plan to use 'observers' in the field, one for each side. In reality, the observers were just JLMC staff members, but Dunlop's hunch soon proved correct. Because the observers were viewed as less threatening than an official mediator, people in Seabury were willing to talk to them. The observers, meanwhile, gained a far more objective analysis of the situation on the ground than they might have gotten otherwise, thus helping the committee chart a more constructive course of action. It was a classic Dunlop "fix," says Brock. "He enjoyed inventing things like that that would contribute to solving problems, but also being misunderstood by people in a constructive way."[23]

The Seabury case was typical, says Brock, in that it presented Dunlop with an intellectual challenge akin to a chess game. Resolving the specific dispute there and laying the groundwork for better future relations required the creation of new tools which could then be utilized when the next case arose. In addition to being able to draw upon his deep knowledge of labor relations, not to mention union foibles, the JLMC also required a knowledge of politics, from the mayors of the cities and towns with which the committee worked, to the state legislature, all the way up to the governor. "It wasn't unlike being secretary of labor," says Brock, who would go on to set up a dispute resolution mechanism based on the structure of the JLMC that would successfully resolve whistleblower conflicts at the Hanford Nuclear site in Washington state. He credits Dunlop for helping him understand and learn to negotiate the political aspects of public sector dispute resolution. "Because I was trained by John, I understood that I had to work at those two levels."[24]

TRANSFORMATION

One measure of the JLMC's effectiveness can be found in the extent to which it transformed the individuals who were part of it. By bringing together a diverse group of people in the interest of solving a complex problem, the "mechanism" exerted a powerful influence. Moschos and Captain Alward, who had started out as adversaries, developed a close bond, and would often speak together to municipal and union groups about the experiment in which they were participating. Long-time Committee staff member Jim Costello says that Dunlop "fashioned my character as much as he taught me about labor relations."[25] A carpenter by trade, Costello recalls that prior to going to work for the JLMC, he took pride in being recognized as an aggressive guy. His experience working along Dunlop taught him a different way to approach disagreements, transforming his demeanor and his way of thinking, says Costello. "To this day, no matter the issue, I have my opinion, but in my head, I automatically go to the side that I have a problem with and then I try to look at where they're coming from. What happens is that that tones your emotions down. I don't get in as much trouble as I used to, with the old Jim Costello, the aggressive guy."[26]

During their years of municipal problem solving together, Dunlop and Costello formed a personal bond as close as father and son. When Dunlop was taken to the hospital on what would be the last day of his life, Costello rushed to the emergency room to see him. That very week the two had attended the JLMC's weekly meeting, followed by a mediation session. "He was just tireless. I mean even at the end of his life, he was still working away," recalls Costello.[27]

And yet Costello's relationship with his mentor got off to something of a rocky start. Soon after taking the staff position at the JLMC, Costello was asked to report on the progress of a particular case to Dunlop at the weekly staff meeting. He did as requested, and several weeks later, when Dunlop grilled him on the case's status, Costello proceeded to pass on the same information he'd delivered previously. "What a mistake," Costello recalls. "He took me apart."[28]

To teach Costello a lesson, Dunlop put on a performance for the whole meeting. What color was the room they were sitting in? Dunlop wanted to know. "Everybody in that room knew that it was painted white. But he was telling me and everybody else that the room was green. We were all looking round saying 'geez, this room doesn't look green to me.'" The lesson being imparted, says Costello, was that Dunlop wouldn't stand for bullshit. "He wanted to send a signal to me that 'you're not going to bluff your way through with me, buddy,'" recalls Costello. "I learned my lesson. He wouldn't ask you a question unless he thought you knew the answer. And if you didn't know the answer, whoa, whoa, whoa…"[29]

SUCCESS METRICS

The JLMC was launched in 1977, and granted permanent status by statute in 1979, in an effort to improve the state of labor-management relations in Massachusetts. Dunlop and others who were involved in the creation of the mechanism sought, not just to get around the negative consequences of last-best-offer arbitration, but to find a better, faster way of resolving disputes. If it worked as its architects intended, the JLMC would make dispute resolution less expensive, less litigious, and more broadly, improve the both the outcomes and relationships resulting from municipal police and fire collective bargaining. When Brock began work on his book-length study, there were already four years of data by which to assess the JLMC's progress, collected and analyzed in part by the body's own researchers.

In its first years, the JLMC made significant progress towards realizing its goals. Settlements were being reached at a rate twice as fast as under the previous system, while significantly more agreements were being reached through mediation than by arbitration. Litigation was down, as was third party arbitration, while face-to-face bargaining, another goal, had increased as well. As Brock determined, the JLMC also made strides toward reaching the framer's larger goals: more mutually acceptable settlements, more problem solving, more structural change in bargaining relationships and the strengthening of bargaining skills on the management side. Writes Brock: "Indications are that the increase in bargaining and the existence of a central, skilled, and respected agency is providing avenues for more mutually acceptable bargaining outcomes than was possible under the more rigid and legalistic arbitration system that previously prevailed."[30] By 2003, the Committee had settled 1,500 disputes by agreement of all of the parties.

In the assessment of the JLMC that Dunlop included in his 1984 volume on dispute resolution, he clearly viewed the experiment as an unbridled success. Designed by the same parties that had to live under the agreements that it facilitated, the JLMC had not only survived a changing political and economic climate, reflected in shifting issues at the negotiating tables, it had evolved in positive, even innovative directions along the way. "The Committee seeks to enhance the agreement-making process," wrote Dunlop. "[I]t is relentless and dogged in its pursuit of new methods to agreement."[31]

By one important metric, however, the JLMC would fall well short of what Dunlop had in mind for it. Despite its measurable success at confronting a problem faced by some 25 other states, the mechanism was never adopted beyond Massachusetts. "I think Dunlop was disappointed by that because it had so much potential value," says Brock.[32] He attributes the failure of the idea to take off, at least in part to Dunlop's own lack of interest in selling it. With the exception of presenting at occasional conferences, Dunlop was far more interested in the hands-on work of actually solving problems than he was in promoting his creation.

There was another reason why the JLMC never caught on as a model, says Brock. Mayors and their staffers didn't like a mechanism that they saw as diminishing their authority, even though they would be gaining more control over police and fire operations as well as costs. "This opposition by the entrenched interests in municipal labor relations made such a cooperative mechanism a tough sell," concludes Brock.[33]

Still, of all of Dunlop's problem-solving forays, the JLMC ranks as the longest running. With the same partisan divides and anti-tax fever that gave rise to the urgent need for creative problem solving in Massachusetts ascendant across the US once again, this experiment would seem to hold out more promise than ever. By taking a complex political dilemma and establishing a non-governmental process for dealing with it, Dunlop figured out a way to give local officials and union leaders the space and political cover to work their way to a solution. Brock remains convinced that Dunlop's approach holds out significant promise, especially with respect to problems that government has essentially "punted" its responsibility to solve. Concludes Brock: "Certainly, political polarization circumscribes opportunities, especially at the Federal level, but Dunlop's approach offers opportunities still that few other approaches can."[34]

NOTES

1. This chapter draws extensively from Jonathan Brock's book *Bargaining Beyond Impasse: Joint Resolution of Public Sector Labor Disputes*, a volume he wrote with John Dunlop's assistance and encouragement.
2. Jonathan Brock, *Bargaining Beyond Impasse: Joint Resolution of Public Sector Labor Disputes* (Boston: Auburn House Publishing Company, 1982) 30.
3. Brock, email correspondence with author, May 8, 2017.
4. Jim Costello, interviewed by the author, July 13, 2016.
5. Ibid.
6. Demetrios Moschos, interviewed by the author, December 21, 2016.
7. Ibid.
8. "Memorandum of Understanding," September 19, 1977. Cited in Brock, 257–260.
9. Brock, 46.

10. As Brock notes, the fire fighters were largely in charge of the political operation, causing some resentment among the police unions. The delay in police involvement caused some resentment, and one union, the Boston Police Association, would oppose the legislation.
11. Bruce E. Kaufman. "Reflections on Six Decades in Industrial Relations: An Interview with John Dunlop." *Industrial and Labor Relations Review*, 55, no. 2 (January 2002): 348.
12. A vice-chairperson position was added in 1979 when the statute was revised.
13. Moschos interview.
14. Ibid.
15. Ibid.
16. Brock, 59.
17. John T. Dunlop, *Dispute Resolution: Negotiation and Consensus Building*. (Boston: Auburn House Publishing Company, 1984) 246.
18. Ibid.
19. Costello interview.
20. Jon Brock, interviewed by the author, December 19, 2016.
21. Ibid.
22. Moschos interview.
23. Brock interview.
24. Ibid.
25. Costello interview.
26. Ibid.
27. Ibid.
28. Ibid.
29. Ibid.
30. Brock, 171–191.
31. Dunlop, *Dispute Resolution*, p. 246–247.
32. Brock email correspondence.
33. Ibid.
34. Ibid.

Conclusion

A Many Storied Life

"Only John could assemble a crew as motley as yourselves," Reverend Peter Gomes told the crowd of well-wishers who gathered at Harvard's Memorial Church on December 12, 2003.[1] John Dunlop had died at the age of 89 two months before, and it had taken nearly that long to plan an event that could pay tribute to the many strands of his work and life. Gomes, an esteemed preacher who held the title of Pusey Minister at the church, mused to the crowd in Brahmin-inflected tones that Dunlop would likely have been pleased to imagine such a gathering taking place on his behalf. They were at Harvard, the institution to which Dunlop had devoted so much of his career, gathered in a church whose construction was completed just a few years before he arrived. But Gomes suspected that the occasion itself would have met with its honoree's approval.

The crowd that filled the pews of Memorial Church was there to recollect what Gomes called "a many storied life." There was former Harvard President Derek Bok, paying tribute to the colleague, friend and co-author who, on more than one occasion, had saved the university from "anarchy." There was his co-conspirator Fred Abernathy who'd joined him on a decades-long quest to fix ailing American industries. Baldemar Velásquez, the firebrand preacher and farmworker organizer was there to tell the story of how the man he called "El Professor" had ventured into the cucumber and tomato fields of northwest Ohio in order to help usher farmworkers from sharecropping to a decent existence. Kris Rondeau, the head of the union representing Harvard's workers, described Dunlop's dedication to seeing the university's overwhelmingly female workforce receive the compensation and respect they were owed, a view that set him apart from many of his contemporaries at

Harvard. Dunlop's long-time labor colleagues, the AFL-CIO's Tom Donahue and Bill Usery, Dunlop's replacement as secretary of labor in the Ford Administration, were present, alongside corporate leaders like Visteon's Peter Pestillo. Dunlop's memorial, like his life, was a joint labor-management affair.

The remembrances that were shared were all distinct, and yet in an important respect the stories that Dunlop's friends, students and colleagues told were essentially the same. However they happened to meet John Dunlop—in a classroom, at a negotiating table or a problem-solving forum—he had mentored them. As Dunlop's former student Richard Freeman explained, "mentoring" in this case went well beyond the traditional definition of a professor leading a student intellectually. "There was a sense that you should be working to solve problems," recalled Freeman.[2] He'd been challenged by Dunlop to look beyond the narrow confines of what the economics profession considered important and to think about how to use his particular skills to work for "the good." And while Dunlop had a particular interest in his graduate students, he routinely issued that challenge to those around him, whether in Harvard's halls or a union hall. "It really didn't matter who you were," said Freeman.[3]

The "motley crew" that paid its respects to Dunlop included many of his former "apprentices," the individuals he'd taught and nurtured, some of them for decades. Jimmy Costello, the rough-edged carpenter who came to know Dunlop through the public sector dispute resolution mechanism known as the Joint Labor Management Committee, was among them. Healthcare executive Karen Ignagni was too. Dunlop had become her mentor when she was a young staffer at the AFL-CIO, a mentorship that essentially continued in some form or other until his death. Ignagni and Costello were joined by former students of Dunlop's, including David Weil, who would follow in his mentor's footsteps, taking over for him as head of the Dunlop Commission, the independent labor relations board established to handle the complex problems of farmworkers, then assuming a leadership position at the Department of Labor. Regardless of the circumstances under which they encountered Dunlop, he had shaped their trajectories, whether enlisting them in his own problem-solving initiatives or advising them on their future steps.

"My development has in large part to do with sitting at [Dunlop's] feet, then at his elbow, then, for a time, at his side as he would take on these extraordinarily difficult tasks," recalls John Read, the Harvard student who served with Dunlop on the Committee of Fifteen, the body tasked with determining the appropriate punishment for Harvard students who'd occupied University Hall.[4] Read's selection was thanks to the chance drawing of a green marble, a process Dunlop himself had suggested. Or was it chance? "I wouldn't be surprised if John had orchestrated that too," says Read, who would follow Dunlop to the Cost of Living Council and the Department of

Labor, and considers their connection to have been the most important of his professional life. "I've carried a green marble with me to this day."[5]

BUILDING HUMAN RELATIONSHIPS

The previous chapters detailed some of Dunlop's many forays into problem solving, with a particular attention to the mechanisms he established in an effort to resolve future disputes, long after the initial emergency had passed. But beneath the structures he was so fond of, and the somewhat clinical language of his field—neutrals and arbitrators, tripartite bodies and collective bargaining—was a profound commitment to human relationships. Whether the conflict that presented itself was unwinding wage and price controls, guiding Harvard back from the brink, or securing benefits for undocumented farmworkers, Dunlop began by focusing on the individuals involved, and more importantly, the connections between them, deploying the sort of deep listening skills for which he was well known.

In the guide to dispute resolution, negotiation and consensus building that he published in 1984, Dunlop referred to this element of his work as "the personal ingredient."[6] This factor of "personality, experience, skill, chemistry, attitude, demeanor, as well as status in the organization" was the most difficult to generalize, Dunlop conceded. And yet he believed that these personal relationships were pivotal. The framework he offered up for practitioners seeking to replicate his style of negotiating concludes with a somewhat anodyne observation about personalities. "The personalities of negotiators and the way they relate to one another does affect the outcome in some instances."[7] This is something of an understatement. The long-term solutions Dunlop sought simply weren't possible without an understanding of the people caught up in the specific problem.

It's easy to view the two major realms of Dunlop's professional life—his career as an academic economist and his problem solving and dispute resolution work—as being largely separate. On the one hand there was Harvard and the world of academic economics, on the other, there was the real world of policy and labor relations problems: Washington DC, labor unions and a Rolodex full of industry leaders. But Dunlop's "systems" thinking applied to both aspects of his work, as an academic who drew from economics, sociology and industrial relations, and as a practitioner who focused upon making institutions, labor unions chief among them, work better for the individuals who operated within them. Revisit the guest lecture that Dunlop delivered to Ray Goldberg's class at the Harvard Business School in 1990, for example, and you can hear him walking the students through his deliberations regarding the dynamics of multiple institutions. Who needed to be at the table? How much authority and respect did the various institutional chiefs actually have? The diagram Dunlop sketched out on the chalkboard rendered the complex dynamics of the farmworkers struggle as a system, representing, as he explained to the students, "the totality of life." Touch one part, he cautioned them, and you touch the whole.[8]

"John had an amazing ability to think about the individuals as they related to the problem he was seeking to solve," says David Weil.[9] "But he was also very much focused on how he could help develop those individuals." This too can be heard in Dunlop's guest lecture. His musing aloud regarding the character of FLOC organizer Baldemar Velásquez wasn't just speculation about whether he could successfully transition from firebrand protest leader to the administrator of a union representing thousands of workers. Dunlop was already thinking about ways that he might assist in the of Velásquez's development. Here too there was an important overlap between Dunlop's academic life and his problem-solving work. Mentoring is expected within the academy. The graduate students who studied with him and conducted research under his guidance were following a traditional path. But Dunlop applied that same tradition to many of the individuals he encountered outside of Harvard. Says Weil: "He believed deeply in what was a kind of apprenticeship. He was committed to helping people develop skills but also to working with them to think through their next steps."[10]

For Velásquez that meant a years-long apprenticeship, during which he learned from Dunlop the art of negotiating, including how to establish the human connections out of which respect, understanding and compromise can emerge, even in a context as fraught and complicated as the farmworkers' struggle. Among the lessons that Velásquez learned from his mentor at the negotiating table: that skillful negotiating requires both patience and motion. "You couldn't help but learn from his constant movement," recalls Velásquez. Dunlop knew "when to cajole, when to encourage, when to pressure, when to compromise, and when to inspire in the face of overwhelming differences."[11]

Just as Dunlop brought the tradition of academic mentoring into his problem-solving work, he also insisted that his academic charges venture beyond the classroom and the library so that they could understand the complexities of the real world and its institutions. Richard Freeman recalls presenting Dunlop with a paper he'd written on labor economics only to have his advisor send him to Washington so that he could learn a thing or two about how the world really worked. In a profession designed to narrow its practitioner's focus, Dunlop urged him to look beyond the tenets of their field. "He sent people off in different directions and gave you a certain view that some things were important. There was a breadth that I saw nowhere else in my academic career," says Freeman.[12]

Dunlop's commitment to mentoring as part of problem solving is perfectly encapsulated in his long-running involvement in the effort by the largely female clerical and technical workforce at Harvard to gain recognition of their union, followed by a first collective bargaining agreement. There was the young union organizer, Kris Rondeau, whom he took under his wing, determined to teach her about the way that Harvard worked. "You've got to understand institutions," Rondeau recalls Dunlop telling her on more than one occasion.[13] Because contract negotiations involved a substantial number of Harvard employees who were brand new to unions, let alone bargaining, Dunlop and Rondeau incorporated professional development into the negotiating process. Here, Dunlop's concept of developing individuals in order that they might play more effective roles in longer term problem solving within their unions or institutions, was applied across an entire university workforce.

Dunlop approached his interactions with Rondeau and HUCTW, Harvard's new union, as a teacher. "His teacherly attitudes suffused everything," recalls Rondeau.[14] And yet it's also clear from his own writings and talks that *he* was "developed" through his involvement with HUCTW. Rondeau's approach to union organizing, one that relied on relationships and trust building, was substantially different from the union cultures with which Dunlop was familiar—the assorted "brotherhoods" in construction, manufacturing and transportation that dominated the AFL-CIO. But the free-wheeling, participatory nature of HUCTW's negotiations with Harvard, seemingly a world away from the closed-door sessions of, say, the Labor-Management Committee, transformed Dunlop's own view of the importance of democracy in problem-solving work.

Suspicious by nature of top-down solutions and technocratic overreach, here he had an opportunity to see rank-and-file clerical and technical workers at Harvard, many of whom had labored without voice or power, blossom into full-fledged union leaders. Not long after HUCTW and Harvard wrapped up contract and negotiations, Dunlop and Rondeau would travel to DC together in an effort to convince AFL-CIO leaders that adopting Rondeau's approach to organizing might be a way to halt the labor movement's downward slide. "It wasn't something they were interested in hearing," recalls Rondeau.[15]

PERSONAL SOLUTIONS

In Dunlop's final days as secretary of labor, he made a point of meeting with his assorted charges in order to help them determine their next steps. While "I don't give advice" was one of his regular refrains, he took a particular interest in guiding both his graduate students and the young staffers who'd accompanied him to Washington. One of his last meetings was with his then secretary, Helen Knox, who was responsible for overseeing his calendar as well as transcribing the audio journal he kept while in office. Dunlop had a full evening of meetings lined up, but "wanted to walk [Knox] through what her plans should be for the period ahead so as to remove some of the uncertainty that has no doubt seriously affected her."[16]

That Dunlop was as concerned about his administrative assistant as he was with the young staffers who'd served with him under both Ford and Nixon, might seem surprising. But it is indicative of what Freeman describes as the sense of democracy that informed Dunlop's work and connections with the individuals in his various worlds. His personal journal also reflects a forward-thinking view on gender that was striking for the time. Again and again he commented on the need for more gender diversity within particular government agencies, or singled out an individual whom he wants to assist with her advancement. "He was a modern man," says Rondeau. "The bowtie was deceiving."[17]

The attention to individuals within a larger institution, regardless of where they ranked in the pecking order, served an additional purpose for Dunlop. Seeing an institution through the eyes of, say, its administrative assistants, gave him an invaluable glimpse into how it worked—and how it could be made to work better. At Harvard, for example, Dunlop came to understand the transformation in the nature of administrative work through the insight of another long serving administrative assistant, Marie Stroud. Word processing and the advent of email were remaking the jobs of the executive assistants who were assigned to senior faculty members. And yet the hierarchical power dynamic so typical of old Harvard remained; the secretaries often sat out in front of a professor's door.

Dunlop worked with a group of administrative assistants to create a pool of employees who shared the work of the Department of Economics. The new arrangement was meant to be a fix for a specific problem: some staffers had too much work, others too little. But it also addressed an institutional inequity at Harvard. A system in which individual faculty members had "their person" was ripe for abuse. Pooling labor introduced a new level of transparency about how individuals at Harvard were being treated. Professors who'd made a practice of sending their assistants out on personal errands, for example, were now subject to scrutiny. The new system also brought with it additional opportunities for professional development—a necessity at a time when office technology was undergoing rapid transformation.

David Weil, who was working with Dunlop on the massive retail and textile industry project during this same time period, says that his response to the secretarial labor dilemma reflected a key ingredient found in virtually all of his problem solving. "He didn't think you could really understand how an organization worked from a distance. In order to really get at the facts, you had to get your hands dirty on the ground."[18] Relatedly, no solution to an institutional problem was workable, especially for the long term, without the commitment and participation of the people within that institution. The same skepticism Dunlop brought to the problem of over-regulation also infused his problem-solving work, says Weil. "He would never lose sight of the fact that in an organization or a bureaucracy, people have constituencies, even if they work for you. It's why you can't just impose a solution from above."[19]

GREATER GOOD

President Ford, in his remarks at Dunlop's swearing in as secretary of labor, praised him as being "uniquely skilled in obtaining practical solutions to the most complex of problems."[20] To view a problem through Dunlop's eyes—whether it was wage and price controls under Nixon, the absence of workplace protections for farmworkers, or the need for a new work arrangement for secretaries at Harvard—was to see the world in all of its complexity. Indeed, Dunlop thrilled to the intellectual challenge of grappling with a deeply complex dilemma. He was outspoken about this, reminding his colleagues with regularity that he wasn't interested in problems that could be solved by "getting out of bed in the morning." Weil argues that Dunlop's insistence on only taking on issues of the five-to-ten years variety spoke to the historian in him. "He took a long view of things. You're not just trying to solve the problem in front of you but educate people and change the way they think," says Weil.[21]

But was there a moral component to the work that Dunlop did? While he may not have used the language of social justice, the emphasis on some kind of greater good pervaded his problem-solving efforts as well as his work as an academic economist. It can be found in the way that he pushed graduate students to think beyond the narrow questions of their academic discipline. It is the reason why Dunlop insisted on forever working in references to "the cucumbers and tomatoes," reminding colleagues far from the growing fields of Northwest Ohio to keep their challenges in perspective. And it explains his tireless efforts to help resolve Harvard's labor dispute with its own workforce. The institution he loved was threatened, and a complex situation demanded a long-term solution, but here was an opportunity to do better by the female clerical and technical workers who'd been treated shabbily, often by his own colleagues.

Dunlop brought his distinctive style to all of the challenges before him: "coolness of judgment, strategic ability and the firmness of will needed to cope with the situation," as Derek Bok describes.[22] But there was also deep commitment to making the world a better place. Dunlop's upbringing as the son of Calvinist missionaries shaped him in profound ways. He inherited a view that all problems were surmountable by hard work even as the work itself was motivated by an understanding that life had a larger purpose. It was the Calvinist in him, though, that would have resisted a discussion of his contribution to the world in such terms—indeed, to being made the object of scrutiny at all.

"John wasn't comfortable being thanked or fussed over," Bok told the gathering at Memorial Church in his farewell to his friend and colleague of nearly a half century. "What he enjoyed was building human relationships, bringing order out of chaos, creating procedures, structures, and relationships to avoid future conflict."[23]

NOTES

1. Reverend Peter Gomes, John T. Dunlop Memorial Service, Memorial Church, Cambridge, MA, December 12, 2003.
2. Ibid.
3. Ibid.
4. John Read, interviewed by the author, September 7, 2016.
5. Ibid.
6. John T. Dunlop, *Dispute Resolution: Negotiation and Consensus Building* (Dover, MA: Auburn House Publishing 1984) 20–21.
7. Ibid.
8. Video recording of Ray Goldberg class, September 26, 1990.
9. David Weil, interviewed by the author, September 11, 2017.
10. Ibid.
11. Baldemar Velásquez, Dunlop Memorial Service.
12. Richard Freeman, Dunlop Memorial Service.
13. Kris Rondeau, interviewed by the author, March 15, 2016.
14. Ibid.
15. Ibid.
16. Diary of John Dunlop, Sec. 16, p. 93.
17. Rondeau interview.
18. Weil interview.
19. Ibid.
20. President Gerald Ford, "Swearing-In of John Dunlop As Secretary of Labor," March 18, 1975.
21. Weil interview.
22. Derek Bok, Dunlop Memorial Service.
23. Ibid.

References

Abernathy, Frederick, John Dunlop, Janice Hammond and David Weil, *A Stitch in Time* (Oxford: Oxford University Press, 1999).

Barger, W.K and Ernesto Reza, *The Farm Labor Movement in the Midwest*, (Austin, TX: University of Texas Press, 1994).

"Big Labor Strives to Break Out of Its Rut," *Fortune*, August 27, 1979, 33.

Brock, Jonathan, *Bargaining Beyond Impasse: Joint Resolution of Public Sector Labor Disputes* (Boston: Auburn House Publishing Company, 1982).

Cowan, Edward, "Dunlop Sees Significant Rise in Phase IV Prices," *The New York Times*, July 13, 1973.

———, "Mandatory Wage Price Controls Ended Except In Food, Health, Building Fields; Nixon Calls for Voluntary Compliance," *New York Times*, January 12, 1973.

———, "Raising Prices Appears Easier," *New York Times*, January 27, 1973.

———, "Wage-Price Missionary," *New York Times*, October 7, 1973.

Dark, Taylor, *Unions and the Democrats: an Enduring Alliance*, (Ithaca, NY: ILR Press, 1999).

Davis, Mike, *Prisoners of the American Dream: Politics and Economy in the History of the US Working Class*, (New York: Verso, 1986).

Dembart, Lee, "Issue and Debate," *New York Times*, November 6, 1975.

U.S. Department of Labor, U.S Department of Commerce, The Dunlop Commission on the Future of Worker-Management Relations, Final Report, John T. Dunlop, December 1, 1994.

———, Fact Finding Report: Dunlop Commission on the Future of Worker-Management Relations, John T. Dunlop, May 1994.

John T. Dunlop, "The Commission and Alternative Dispute Resolution," Paper presented at the Society of Professionals in Dispute Resolution conference, October 24, 1996, Anaheim, CA.

———, *Dispute Resolution: Negotiation and Consensus Building* (Dover, MA: Auburn House Publishing, 1984).

———, *Industrial Relations Systems*, (Boston: Harvard Business School Press, 1993).

———, *The Management of Labor Unions*, (Lexington, MA, Lexington Books, 1990).

———, personal diary, April 6, 1975–February 26, 1976.

———, "Policy Decisions and Research in Economic and Industrial Relations," Industrial and Labor Relations Review, 30, no. 3, (April, 1977): 275–282.

———, "Some Recollections of a Brief Tenure," *Monthly Labor Review*. 111, no 2 (February 1988), 46–49.

——— and Richard D. Bartel, "Working Towards Consensus," *Challenge*, 25, no. 3 (1982), pp. 26–34.

Edsall, Thomas Byrd, *The New Politics of Inequality*, (New York: W.W. Norton, 1985).

Engelmayer, Jean E. and Melissa I. Weissberg, "Reflecting on the 1969 Student Strike," *Harvard Crimson*, April 9, 1984.
Doug Fraser's Resignation Letter from the Labor-Management Group, *Daily Labor Report*, no. 139, July 17, 1978.
Galeota, William and William Kutik, "Students Occupy University Hall, Eject Deans, Staff, from Offices," *Harvard Crimson*, April 9, 1969.
Gammill, Marion, "A Struggle for Empowerment," *Harvard Crimson*, May 19, 1993.
Greenhouse, Steven, "Controversial Overtime Rules Take Effect," The New York Times, August 23, 2004.
"Harvard University Union, Management Have Working Relationship, Parties Say," *Labor Relations Week*, April 11, 1990, 357.
Hoerr, John, *We Can't Eat Prestige: The Women Who Organized Harvard*, (Philadelphia: Temple University Press, 1997).
Hurd, Richard, "Organizing and Representing Clerical Workers: The Harvard Model," in Women and Unions, ed. Dorothy Sue Cobble, (Ithaca: ILR Press, 1993), 316–336.
Kaufman, Bruce, "Reflections on Six Decades in Industrial Relations: An Interview with John Dunlop." *Industrial and Labor Relations Review*, 55, no. 2 (January 2002): 324–348.
Kennedy, Michael, "Migrant Farmworkers in the Midwest," case study, (Boston: Harvard Business Publishing, 1985.)
Kochan, Thomas A., *Shaping the Future of Work*, (New York: Business Expert Press, 2016).
Lerer, Justin,"Yard Watches Students Seize University Hall," *Harvard Crimson*, June 3, 1977.
Liptak, Kevin, "Trump: 'Nobody knew health care could be so complicated,'" CNN, February 28. 2017.
Linder, Marc, *Wars of Attrition: Vietnam, the Business Roundtable and the Decline of Construction Unions*, (Iowa City, Iowa: Fanpihua Press, 2000).
Lubow, Arthur, "Dunlop Resigns to Take Nixon Post," *Harvard Crimson*, January 11, 1973.
"Offner's Sentence," Harvard Crimson, May 19, 1969.
Palladino, Grace, *Skilled Hands, Strong Spirits: A Century of Building Trades History*, (Ithaca, NY: Cornell University Press, 2005).
Penn, Mark, "John Dunlop Will Return to Harvard When Washington Post Ends," *Harvard Crimson*, June 10, 1974.
Raskin, A.H., "Concessions in Labor's Pragmatic Stance," *The New York Times*, June 15, 1977.
Reyes, Teófilo, "8000 'Guest Workers' Join Farm Union in North Carolina," Labor Notes, September 30, 2004.
Riesel, Victor, "Dunlop Labor's Choice for Job," syndicated column, March 28, 1975.
Rosenbaum, David "Energy and Construction-Picket Bills are Approved," *New York Times*, December 16, 1975.
Rosenblatt, Roger, *Coming Apart: A Memoir of the Harvard Wars of 1969*, (Boston: Little, Brown, 1997).
Shabecoff, Philip, "Attacks Mount on Ford Economic Policy," *New York Times*, November, 24, 1974.
———, "House Rejects Bill on Picketing Sites by Building Unions," *New York Times,* March 23, 1977.
Shay, Matthew, "Overregulation: Undermining America's Economic Engine," *The Hill*, May 3, 2016.
Shultz, George, "John Dunlop," *Proceedings of the American Philosophical Society* 150, no. 1, (March 2006): 187–190.
Silk, Leonard, "Inflation Fighters Tripartite Forum," *New York Times,* July 4th, 1977.
Swanson, Daniel, "Good-Bye John: An Adversary Departs," *Harvard Crimson*, June 14, 1973.
Swoboda, Frank, "Autoworker Pullout Signals Labor Strife," *Washington Post*, July 21, 1978.
———, "Labor Commission's Head Looks at Unshackling Cooperation on the Job," *Washington Post*, July 4, 1993.
"Too Much Regulation Has Piled up in America," *The Economist*, March 2, 2017.
Vinik, Danny, "Trump's War on Regulations is Real. But is it Working?" Politico, January 20, 2018.

Walker, William N., "Forty Years After the Freeze," unpublished manuscript, November 2011, https://nixonswageandpricefreeze.files.wordpress.com/2011/07/forty-years-after-the-freeze.pdf.

Zack, Arnold, "The Due Process Protocol: Getting There and Getting Over It," *Employee Rights and Employment Policy Journal*, 11, no. 2 (2007): 101–110.

Index

About the Author

Jennifer C. Berkshire's reporting and commentary on labor, education, and politics have appeared in the *New Republic*, the *Washington Post*, the *Baffler*, and other publications. Berkshire discovered her passion for interviewing while covering a series of bitter labor battles that wracked her native Midwest in the early 1990s. She teaches journalism at Boston College and at the Labor Center at UMass Amherst.

www.ingramcontent.com/pod-product-compliance
Ingram Content Group UK Ltd.
Pitfield, Milton Keynes, MK11 3LW, UK
UKHW041142300926
15471UKWH00011B/94

9 780761 872597